LEADING A

High Reliability School™

ROBERT J. MARZANO
PHILIP B. WARRICK
CAMERON L. RAINS
RICHARD DUFOUR

Foreword by Jeffrey C. Jones

Solution Tree | Press

a division of
Solution Tree

555 North Morton Street
Bloomington, IN 47404
800.733.6786 (toll free) / 812.336.7700
FAX: 812.336.7790

email: info@SolutionTree.com
SolutionTree.com

Visit **go.SolutionTree.com/leadership** to download the free reproducibles in this book.

Printed in the United States of America

Library of Congress Cataloging-in-Publication Data

Names: Marzano, Robert J., author.
Title: Leading a high reliability school / Robert J. Marzano, Phil Warrick,
    Cameron L. Rains, and Richard DuFour ; foreword by Jeffrey C. Jones.
Description: Bloomington, IN : Solution Tree Press, [2018] | Includes
    bibliographical references and index.
Identifiers: LCCN 2017049716 | ISBN 9781945349348 (perfect bound)
Subjects: LCSH: School improvement programs. | Teacher effectiveness. |
    Professional learning communities.
Classification: LCC LB2822.8 .M388 2018 | DDC 371.2/07--dc23 LC record available at
https://lccn.loc.gov/2017049716

Solution Tree
Jeffrey C. Jones, CEO
Edmund M. Ackerman, President

Solution Tree Press
President and Publisher: Douglas M. Rife
Editorial Director: Sarah Payne-Mills
Art Director: Rian Anderson
Managing Production Editor: Kendra Slayton
Senior Production Editor: Christine Hood
Senior Editor: Amy Rubenstein
Copy Editor: Jessi Finn
Proofreader: Evie Madsen
Text and Cover Designer: Laura Cox

Acknowledgments

We would like to extend our gratitude and appreciation to all the staff members in high reliability schools and those working toward high reliability with whom we have been fortunate enough to collaborate. Keep up the great work you are doing on behalf of students.

Visit **go.SolutionTree.com/leadership** to download the free reproducibles in this book.

Table of Contents

Chapter 5

Chapter 6

Chapter 7

Appendix

About the Authors

 **Robert J. Marzano, PhD,** is the cofounder and chief academic officer of Marzano Research in Denver, Colorado. During his fifty years in the field of education, he has worked with educators as a speaker and trainer and has authored more than forty books and two hundred articles on topics such as instruction, assessment, writing and implementing standards, cognition, effective leadership, and school intervention. His books include *The New Art and Science of Teaching, Leaders of Learning, Making Classroom Assessments Reliable and Valid, A Handbook for Personalized Competency-Based Education,* and *Teacher Evaluation That Makes a Difference.* His practical translations of the most current research and theory into classroom strategies are known internationally and are widely practiced by both teachers and administrators.

Dr. Marzano received a bachelor's degree from Iona College in New York, a master's degree from Seattle University, and a doctorate from the University of Washington.

To learn more about Robert J. Marzano's work, visit marzanoresearch.com.

 **Philip B. Warrick, EdD,** spent the first twenty-five years of his educational career as a teacher, assistant principal, principal, and superintendent and has experience in leading schools in the states of Nebraska and Texas. Dr. Warrick was named 1998 Nebraska Outstanding New Principal of the Year and was the 2005 Nebraska State High School Principal of the Year. He is a past regional president for the Nebraska Council of School Administrators (NCSA). He also served on the NCSA legislative

committee. In 2003, he was one of the initial participants to attend the Nebraska Educational Leadership Institute conducted by The Gallup Corporation at Gallup University in Omaha. In 2008, Dr. Warrick was hired as the campus principal at Round Rock High School in Round Rock, Texas. In 2010, he was invited to be an inaugural participant in the Texas Principals' Visioning Institute, where he collaborated with other principals from the state of Texas to develop a vision for effective practices in Texas schools.

In 2011, Dr. Warrick joined the Solution Tree–Marzano Research team and now works as an author and global consultant in the areas of school leadership, curriculum, instruction, assessment, grading, and collaborative teaming. He earned a bachelor of science from Chadron State College in Chadron, Nebraska, and earned his master's and doctoral degrees from the University of Nebraska-Lincoln.

 **Cameron L. Rains, EdD,** is the assistant superintendent of curriculum and instruction for Clark-Pleasant Community School Corporation. In this role, he is part of a team working to ensure that all students in the district learn at high levels. Previously, Dr. Rains served as a teacher and instructional coach, and he acquired almost ten years of administrative experience as a director of elementary education and director of curriculum and instruction.

Dr. Rains is passionate about school and district leadership and applying research findings in the school environment. He coauthored an article on the importance of reading fluency for *Reading and Writing Quarterly* and is coauthor of the book *Stronger Together: Answering the Questions of Collaborative Leadership.* Dr. Rains also serves as a Marzano Research associate, where he delivers professional development on a wide range of topics across the United States.

Dr. Rains earned a bachelor of science degree in elementary education and a master of science degree in educational leadership from Indiana University. He also holds an educational specialist degree and doctorate in educational leadership from Ball State University.

To learn more about Cameron L. Rains's work, follow him @CameronRains on Twitter.

 **Richard DuFour, EdD,** was a public school educator for thirty-four years, serving as a teacher, principal, and superintendent. During his nineteen-year tenure as both principal and superintendent at Adlai E. Stevenson High School in Lincolnshire, Illinois, Stevenson became one of only three schools in the nation to win the U.S. Department of Education Blue Ribbon Award on four occasions and the first comprehensive high school to be designated a New America High School as a model of successful school reform. Dr. DuFour received his state's highest award as both a principal and superintendent.

A prolific author and sought-after consultant, Dr. DuFour was recognized as one of the leading authorities on helping school practitioners implement the Professional Learning Communities at Work® process in their schools and districts.

Dr. DuFour wrote a quarterly column for the *Journal of Staff Development* for nearly a decade. He was the lead consultant and author of the Association for Supervision and Curriculum Development's video series on principalship and the author of several other videos. He was named as one of the Top 100 School Administrators in North America by *Executive Educator* magazine, was presented the Distinguished Scholar Practitioner Award from the University of Illinois, and was the 2004 recipient of the National Staff Development Council's Distinguished Service Award.

To learn more about Richard DuFour's work, visit AllThingsPLC (www.allthings plc.info).

To book Robert J. Marzano, Philip B. Warrick, or Cameron L. Rains for professional development, contact pd@SolutionTree.com.

Foreword

By Jeffrey C. Jones

Student achievement—this is by far the main purpose of a school. Yet with the rising tide of standardized testing and the numerous demands placed on schools, educators often find themselves straying from this main objective. From daily paperwork to lesson plans and assessment, educators are bombarded with things to do besides focus on learning, and seemingly not enough time to do them. So, how can educators sort through the myriad tasks, both required and optional, to focus on the essential things they need to do to promote student achievement? In other words, how can they determine that the work they're doing is the right work?

In *Leading a High Reliability School*, my friends and authors Bob Marzano, Phil Warrick, and Cameron Rains provide a comprehensive model that leaders can follow to ensure the right work is being done. Grounded in years of research, the high reliability school (HRS) model encompasses twenty-five variables, or leading indicators, that leaders can implement. Ranging from a safe school environment to a guaranteed and viable curriculum for all, these leading indicators provide a road map for leaders to follow.

In the clear and compelling introduction crafted just prior to losing his battle with cancer, our dear friend and colleague Dr. Rick DuFour writes about the powerful impact of professional learning community (PLC) work, specifically the PLC at Work® process and its integral role in creating high reliability schools. A pioneer in PLCs and a Solution Tree author for more than twenty years, Rick brought his decades of experience and insight to this work.

In the remaining chapters, Bob, Phil, and Cameron detail the work surrounding each of the twenty-five leading indicators of a high reliability school. With a wealth of examples, rubrics, learning progressions, and tables, they walk the reader through the process of implementing each indicator, obtaining data for continuous improvement, and ensuring leader accountability. Each chapter concludes with evidence from the field—anecdotes from school leaders about their experiences, challenges, and successes in implementing the HRS model.

The work of schools isn't easy. It involves asking hard questions, prioritizing the work, collaborating, analyzing data, and monitoring progress. The list goes on and on. In *Leading a High Reliability School*, leaders will find a comprehensive model that enables them to approach the work with clarity of purpose and clear direction. And at Solution Tree and Marzano Research, we consider it a great honor to bring this work to you.

Introduction

The Primacy of the PLC Process

By Richard DuFour

• • •

In the subtitle of his 1961 book, *Excellence*, John W. Gardner asks, "Can we be equal and excellent too?" Contemporary educators face the challenge of answering this question in the affirmative. Schools that strive for excellence must take steps to ensure that all students not only have equal access to but also acquire the knowledge, skills, and dispositions that will prepare them for their future. These institutions that were created to sort and select students based on their perceived abilities, socioeconomic status, and likely careers now are called on to ensure every student graduates from high school with the high levels of learning necessary for success in college or other avenues of postsecondary training. In short, a school cannot become excellent unless it commits to equity as well.

The Effective Schools research of the 1970s and 1980s established that some schools more effectively than others help students achieve the intended levels of proficiency. Schools, however, often overlook that student achievement differs significantly more *within* schools than *between* schools largely because of the variability in teacher effectiveness within the same school (Hattie, 2015).

This finding should come as no surprise given that the traditional schooling structure in a large portion of the world has involved individual teachers in isolated classrooms making decisions based on their experience, expertise, preferences, and interests. This structure has subjected students to an educational lottery in which what they learn, how much they learn, how they are assessed, and what happens when they struggle are almost entirely a function of their assigned teacher.

Those who hope to lead a high reliability school (HRS) must confront the challenge of reducing this variability so all students have access to good teaching, a guaranteed and viable curriculum, careful monitoring of their learning, systematic interventions when they struggle, and extension when they demonstrate high levels of proficiency. Their best hope for meeting this challenge lies in making the Professional Learning Communities at Work (PLC at Work) process the cornerstone of HRS creation. In doing so, educators will serve the cause of both excellence and equity.

The PLC at Work Process as the Cornerstone of High Reliability Schools

In order for the HRS model to drive a school toward excellence, educators in the school must know that the professional learning community process represents the foundation of their efforts. We recognize that although the term *PLC* has become ubiquitous, groups apply varying definitions. For our purposes, we want to distinguish among the terms *professional learning community*, *collaborative team*, and *professional learning community process*.

In many schools, educators refer to their collaborative teams as a *PLC*. We discourage this use of the term. A PLC is a school or district that is attempting to implement the PLC process. Many elements of the process require schoolwide coordination that goes beyond the work of a grade-level or course-specific team. The collaborative team, although not a PLC, is the fundamental structure of a PLC and the engine that drives the PLC process.

The PLC process calls for educators to work together collaboratively in recurring cycles of collective inquiry and action research to achieve better results for the students they serve. It operates under the assumption that purposeful, continuous, job-embedded learning for educators is the key to improved student learning. Before delving into the nuances of PLCs, let's consider a fundamental prerequisite to any effective school—providing a safe and orderly environment for both student and adult learning.

The Importance of a Safe and Orderly Environment

When Abraham Maslow (1943) created his hierarchy of needs, he cited *safety* and *orderliness* as fundamental needs second only to biological needs such as air, water, food, and so on. But he found that although addressing safety needs is vital for progressing to higher levels of self-actualization, it does not ensure that progression. The same is true of classrooms.

Every classroom teacher knows the importance of effective classroom management. Individuals with outstanding content knowledge will flounder as teachers if they cannot maintain a safe and orderly classroom. But effective teachers go beyond classroom management to use strategies that engage learners and constantly monitor their learning. Classroom management is a necessary condition for effective teaching, but it is not sufficient on its own.

This same principle applies to schools. Maintaining a safe and orderly environment is important, but it is not nearly enough. Every school leader must ensure a safe and orderly environment for both student and adult learning. But if school leaders seek to create excellent schools, they must move beyond running a tight ship.

Given the significance of a safe and orderly environment, I find it striking how frequently staff members lack knowledge of specific indicators that could provide insight into how to enhance this important aspect of their school. I ask faculty:

- "How many of you know the number of discipline referrals that were written in your school last year?"
- "How many of you know the number-one cause of discipline referrals in your school?"
- "How many of you know the number of student suspensions that occurred in your school last year?"
- "Is there a time of day, day of the week, or place in the school that discipline problems are most likely to arise?"
- "Do students report feeling safe in your school?"
- "Do students report either being bullied or witnessing bullying in your school?"

In most instances, faculty members cannot answer these questions. If they don't have a clue about their current reality, they find it difficult to improve on that reality in any coordinated way. Therefore, school leaders should keep information about the school's environment at the forefront and frequently engage the staff in analyzing the information and identifying potential areas of need and strategies for improvement. One strategy is embracing the three big ideas driving the PLC process.

Assumptions Driving the PLC Process

Three big ideas drive the PLC process (DuFour, DuFour, Eaker, Many, & Mattos, 2016). The extent to which educators consider and embrace these ideas has a significant impact on that process's outcomes in a district or school. These three big ideas include (1) a focus on learning, (2) a collaborative culture, and (3) a results orientation.

A Focus on Learning

The first and biggest of the big ideas states that a school's fundamental purpose is to ensure all students acquire the knowledge, skills, and dispositions that will enable them to continue learning beyond the K–12 system. This represents a radical departure from the traditional premise that school's purpose is merely to give students the opportunity to learn. The mantra of "The teacher's job is to teach, and the student's job is to learn" supports this traditional premise. The relevant question for this premise asks, Was the content taught, or was the curriculum *covered*? If, however, a school's fundamental purpose is to ensure that teachers do not merely teach students but expect them to learn, the relevant question becomes, Did the student learn? Did the student acquire the intended knowledge, skills, and dispositions of this course, unit, or lesson?

In our work with schools in implementing the PLC process, my colleagues and I have found that we can shift thinking on the purpose of school by addressing the four pillars that serve as the foundation of the PLC process: (1) mission, (2) vision, (3) collective commitments, and (4) goals (DuFour et al., 2016).

1. **Mission:** Why does the school exist? What is the fundamental purpose of our school? What have we come together to accomplish?

2. **Vision:** What must we become as a school in order to better fulfill our fundamental purpose? Can we describe the school we hope to become in the next five years? What policies, practices, procedures, and culture align best with a mission of learning for all?

3. **Collective commitments:** How must we behave? What commitments must we make and honor in order to become the school in our vision so we can better fulfill our fundamental purpose? Do our commitments describe in specific terms the behaviors we should demonstrate today to help move our school forward?

4. **Goals:** Which steps will we take and when? What targets and timelines will we establish to mark our progress in becoming the school we have described in our vision? How will we know if our collective efforts are making a difference?

Schools often prefer to avoid these foundational questions and get right to the nuts and bolts of the PLC process. Doing so is a mistake. A school will struggle in its PLC implementation efforts if a faculty persists in believing that its job is to teach rather than to help all students learn, and if staff members have no idea where the school wants to go in its improvement efforts. It will struggle if educators refuse to articulate the commitments they hope will characterize their school and if they have no benchmarks to monitor progress. Therefore, we highly recommend that leaders engage the staff in considering the questions posed in the PLC foundation.

Marcus Buckingham (2005), a global researcher and thought leader, contends that, above all else, leaders of any effective organization must know the importance of clarity. Having clarity means communicating consistently in words and actions the organization's purpose, the future the organization will attempt to create, the specific actions members can immediately take to achieve its goals, and the progress indicators it will track. Engaging the staff in considering the four pillars of the PLC foundation is the key to establishing that clarity.

However, leaders must do more than simply invite people to share opinions. A fundamental prerequisite in decision making in a PLC is building shared knowledge about the most promising practices. In other words, staff members must learn together about the research base and evidence that can help them intelligently answer the PLC foundation questions. Uninformed people make uninformed decisions. Therefore, in building consensus in a PLC, leaders must take responsibility for providing staff with the information they need to make good decisions at all points in the process.

A Collaborative Culture

The second big idea driving the PLC process is that for a school to help all students learn, it must build a collaborative culture in which members take collective responsibility for all students. The traditional mantra of "These are *my* students" gives way to "These are *our* students, and we share the responsibility to ensure their learning." Here again, the issue of equity comes to the fore. What to teach, content sequencing, appropriate pacing, assessment, intervention, extension, and instructional strategies have traditionally come under the individual classroom teacher's purview, which, as previously mentioned, makes equity virtually impossible.

The PLC process calls on collaborative team members to make these decisions collectively rather than in isolation. The entire team decides what students must know and be able to do for the entire course and for each unit within the course. It establishes the content's sequencing and the appropriate pacing for each unit. The team develops common formative assessments for each unit and agrees on the criteria it will use in judging the quality of student work. The team identifies students who need intervention or extension, and the school creates the systems to ensure students receive this additional support in a timely manner. It analyzes transparent evidence of student learning in order to inform and improve its practice. None of this will occur without effective leadership that ensures it puts structures and supports in place to foster effective collaboration. We will address the elements of that leadership later in this introduction.

A Results Orientation

The third big idea that drives the PLC process states that educators must assess their effectiveness on the basis of results rather than intentions. Project-based goals such as "We will integrate technology into our language arts program" and "We will develop six new common assessments" give way to SMART goals that ask educators to focus on how their projects and efforts will impact student achievement. The *SMART* goal acronym helps educators focus on evidence of student learning (Conzemius & O'Neill, 2014). A SMART goal is:

- **Strategic**—The goal aligns with a school or district goal. A team that achieves its SMART goal contributes to the school or district goal.
- **Measurable**—The goal provides a basis of comparison to determine whether evidence of student learning indicates improvement or decline.
- **Attainable**—The goal is realistic enough that team members believe they can achieve it through their collective efforts.
- **Results oriented**—The goal focuses on results rather than activities or intentions. In order to achieve a SMART goal, a team must typically help more students learn at higher levels than in the past.
- **Time bound**—The goal specifies when the team expects to achieve its goal.

Teams can and should create SMART goals for the entire school year and for every unit they teach during the year.

We cannot overemphasize the importance of collective inquiry and open dialogue about the three big ideas for successful implementation of the PLC process. More rigorous standards and more informative assessments cannot, by themselves, improve a school. If educators convince themselves that they fulfill their responsibility simply when they present content, that they work best in isolation, and that they need to use evidence of student learning only to assign grades—rather than to inform professional practice to better meet student needs—even well-designed structures and processes have little impact on student learning. School transformation requires significant changes in the culture of schooling, which, in turn, requires educators to engage in meaningful and informed dialogue about the assumptions, beliefs, and expectations that should drive their work.

Critical Questions for Team and School Consideration

It stands to reason that any school that claims it is committed to helping all students learn must engage collaborative teams in collectively considering certain critical questions. The four critical questions of learning in the PLC process include (DuFour et al., 2016):

1. **What is it we want students to learn?**—What knowledge, skills, and dispositions do we expect each student to acquire at the end of this instructional unit, course, or grade level?
2. **How will we know if students are learning?**—How will we monitor each student's learning during daily instruction and during the unit?

3. **How will we respond when students don't learn?**—What systems do we have in place to provide students who struggle with additional time and support for acquiring essential knowledge, skills, and dispositions?

4. **How will we extend learning for students who are highly proficient?**—What systems do we have in place to extend learning for students who have already learned the essential standards?

In *Collaborative Teams That Transform Schools*, Robert Marzano, Tammy Heflebower, Jan K. Hoegh, Phil Warrick, and Gavin Grift (2016) recommend two additional questions that educators in a high reliability school should consider.

5. **How will we increase our instructional competence?**—What systems are in place to help teachers improve their pedagogical skills?

6. **How will we coordinate our efforts as a school?**—How will we ensure that all initiatives in the school are operating in a cohesive and coherent manner?

Let's compare and contrast how a traditional school and a PLC would attempt to address these six questions.

What Is It We Want Students to Learn?

Marzano's (2003) research in *What Works in Schools* has made the term *guaranteed and viable curriculum* part of the educational lexicon. Thanks to his work, two general understandings persist: (1) effective schools provide students with access to the same curriculum content in a specific course and at a specific grade level, regardless of their assigned teacher; and (2) teachers can teach this curriculum in the amount of instructional time provided. (Chapter 4, page 107, elaborates on the importance of a guaranteed and viable curriculum.)

Traditionally, districts have addressed this key element of effective schooling by creating district curriculum and pacing guides and distributing the appropriate guide to each teacher based on his or her grade level or course. This practice often creates the illusion of a guaranteed and viable curriculum because, theoretically, teachers of the same content work from the same document. Too often, however, the mere distribution of documents has little impact on what actually happens in the classroom. We cannot assume that individual teachers will read the documents, interpret them consistently, apply the same priorities to each curricular standard, devote similar amounts of time to the various standards, and have the ability to teach each standard well. Furthermore, simply distributing documents to teachers does not result in either the teacher clarity or the teacher commitment essential to provide students with a guaranteed and viable curriculum.

As we state in *Leaders of Learning* (DuFour & Marzano, 2011):

> The only way the curriculum in a school can truly be guaranteed is if the teachers themselves, those who are called upon to deliver the curriculum, have worked collaboratively to do the following:
> - Study the intended curriculum.
> - Agree on priorities within the curriculum.
> - Clarify how the curriculum translates into student knowledge and skills.
> - Establish general pacing guidelines for delivering the curriculum.
> - Commit to one another that they will, in fact, teach the agreed-upon curriculum. (p. 91)

States and districts can prescribe an *intended* curriculum, but the *implemented* curriculum—what gets taught when the teacher closes the classroom door—has a bigger impact on the *attained* curriculum—what students actually learn. High reliability schools require the PLC process to establish a rigorous, guaranteed, and viable curriculum that reflects a commitment to both excellence and equity.

How Will We Know If Students Are Learning?

Once again, it stands to reason that a school committed to ensuring high levels of learning for all students would have a process in place to continually monitor and support each student's learning. That process would include strategies that check for student understanding during classroom instruction each day. Team members could work together to enhance each other's strategies for making these ongoing checks. For example, teachers could ask students directed questions focused on content that is critical to students' academic success, have students write short responses or solve problems during observation, and gather signals from students as to their level of understanding using whiteboards, clickers, or exit slips. This daily formative assessment is intended to help teachers assess student understanding and make instructional adjustments. It also alerts students to areas of confusion or misunderstanding so they can seek the appropriate help.

But the cornerstone of the PLC assessment process is team-developed common formative assessments administered at least once during a unit. A team assesses students who are expected to acquire the same knowledge and skills, using the same method and instrument, according to the team's agreed-on criteria for judging the quality of student work.

Extensive research supports the effectiveness of common assessments (Ainsworth, 2014; Battelle for Kids, 2015; Chenoweth, 2009; Christman et al., 2009; Odden & Archibald, 2009; Reeves, 2004). But the research in support of formative assessments is even more compelling. As Dylan Wiliam and Marnie Thompson (2007) conclude, effective use of formative assessments, developed through teacher learning communities, promises not only the largest potential gains in student achievement but also a process for affordable teacher professional development. Marzano (2006) describes formative assessment as "one of the most powerful weapons in a teacher's arsenal. An effective standards-based, formative assessment program can help to dramatically enhance student achievement throughout the K–12 system" (back cover). Also, W. James Popham (2013) writes, "Ample research evidence is now at hand to indicate emphatically that when the formative-assessment process is used, students learn better—lots better" (p. 29).

Unquestionably, team-developed common formative assessments serve the interest of equity because a teacher team, rather than an isolated teacher, establishes questions of assessment types, rigor, and criteria for success. It is important to emphasize, however, that these assessments also serve the purpose of excellence. When teachers have clarity on what they want their students to accomplish and they know how they will ask students to demonstrate their proficiency, they more effectively help students learn.

Furthermore, when teachers use the information from these common formative assessments to examine the impact of their individual and collective practice, they experience a powerful catalyst for instructional improvement. In a PLC, educators use a protocol for examining evidence of student learning. First, team members identify struggling students who need additional time and support for learning. Second, they identify students who demonstrate high proficiency and will benefit from an extended learning opportunity. Providing this intervention and extension is part of a schoolwide plan to better meet the needs of individual students.

The team then turns its attention to the performance of students taught by specific teachers. If a teacher's students have performed particularly well, the team asks the teacher to share strategies, ideas, and materials that contributed to that success. If a teacher's students have struggled, the team offers advice, assistance, and materials to help the teacher improve his or her instruction. The team uses evidence of student learning to promote its members' learning.

As Kerry Patterson and his colleagues find in their study of what influences people to change, "Nothing changes the mind like the hard cold world hitting it in the face with actual real-life data" (Patterson, Grenny, Maxfield, McMillan, & Switzler, 2008, p. 51). Richard Elmore (2006) comes to a similar conclusion, writing, "Teachers have to feel that there is some compelling reason for them to practice differently, with the best direct evidence being that students learn better" (p. 38).

When a collaborative teacher team analyzes the transparent results of a common formative assessment, evidence of student learning speaks for itself. A teacher who genuinely believes his or her students lack the ability to produce quality work can be persuaded to re-examine that assumption when students taught by other team members consistently demonstrate quality. As Elmore (2010) writes, "Adult beliefs about what children can learn are changed by watching students do things that the adults didn't believe that they—the students—could do" (p. 8). Concrete evidence of irrefutably better results acts as a powerful persuader.

Common formative assessments can also bring about change in instructional practice through the power of positive peer pressure. I have never known a teacher who feels indifferent to how peers perceive him or her when it comes to instructional competence. A teacher whose students consistently cannot demonstrate proficiency on common formative assessments will either look for ways to improve instruction or look for a school where a lack of transparency about student learning allows him or her to hide. Unfortunately, many such schools exist.

When a team administers a common formative assessment, another possible outcome may occur. What if no one on the team has the ability to help students demonstrate the intended knowledge or skill? If the team agrees that the skill or concept is indeed essential to student success, and it agrees that its common formative assessment reliably ascertains whether students have become proficient, it becomes incumbent on the team to look to its professional development for teaching the skill or concept more effectively. The team can look to other educators in the school or district, specialists from the central office, coaches, networks of educators, or workshops on the topic. In other words, student learning needs drive professional development.

How Will We Respond When Students Don't Learn?

In even the greatest schools, some students will likely not meet an instructional unit's intended outcomes by the time the unit ends, despite teachers' best efforts and intentions. In a traditional school, in which a single isolated classroom teacher takes sole responsibility for each student's learning, that teacher faces a quandary. On one hand, the curriculum calls for moving forward with new important content, and the teacher hopes to ensure his or her students have access to that content (or an *opportunity to learn*). Most students in the class are ready to proceed. On the other hand, some students cannot demonstrate proficiency in essential prerequisite skills for the next unit. The school has charged the teacher with leaving no student behind, so what does the teacher do? Does the teacher provide most students with busywork for a few days so he or she can attend to those who are struggling? Or should the teacher move on and hope that students lacking prerequisite skills somehow pick them up on their own? Imagine this teacher has a daily class load of more than 150 high school students. Given this scenario, the teacher's job is not difficult—it is impossible.

In a traditional school, the individual classroom teacher must resolve this problem. The disparity with which teachers address the question, What happens when students don't learn? provides one of the best examples of the traditional school model's inherent inequity. Some teachers allow students to retake assessments; others don't. Some teachers provide feedback on student papers or projects before assigning grades; others simply grade the first attempt. Some teachers keep parents informed of students' progress; others won't. Some teachers come early and stay late to assist struggling students; others won't or can't. Some teachers accept late work without penalty; others accept the work but deduct points for tardiness. Still others won't accept late work and assign a zero. Some teachers average scores to determine a final grade; others consider early efforts formative. Perhaps the best evidence of the variety in what teachers do when students struggle is that teachers often appeal for their own children to get assigned to certain teachers while avoiding others.

Educators in a PLC recognize the inherent inequity in the traditional system and work collectively to establish a systematic process for providing students with additional time and support for learning, regardless of students' assigned teachers. The master schedule's purposeful design provides time during the regular school day when students receive this support without missing new direct instruction. The system of interventions relies on frequent, timely monitoring of each student's learning and provides additional time for learning as soon as a student struggles. Students continue to receive this support until they demonstrate proficiency.

Let's apply this premise to the dilemma of the teacher who teaches a unit and then discovers that most students have achieved the intended standard, but a few have not. In a PLC, the teacher would teach the next curricular unit, ensuring that struggling students receive additional time and targeted support. Because the collaborative team has agreed on the unit's essential or priority standard, pacing, and common assessment, the teachers providing intervention know what help students need. The team can say, "These students need help with subtracting two-digit integers," as opposed to, "These students are not doing well in mathematics." When the teachers working with these students have confidence in the students' ability to demonstrate proficiency on the intended skill, they give the students a similar iteration (form B) of the original assessment, and their new scores replace their previous struggling scores.

Traditional schools have operated under the assumption that they have fixed time and support for student learning. Every student will receive sixty minutes of language arts instruction per day for 176 school days. Every student will receive essentially the same amount of the teacher's attention and support. But if time and support for learning remain constants, that will always make learning the variable. Some students will learn given that amount of time and support, and others won't.

In a PLC, because of the collective commitment to high levels of learning for every student, time and support are variables, and learning is the constant. Perhaps most students will master a skill in three weeks of sixty minutes of instruction a day. Others may need four weeks of ninety minutes a day to achieve mastery. Most mission statements do not say, "Our mission is to help all students learn fast and the first time we teach a skill"; they simply say, "Our mission is to help all students learn." In order to stay true to that mission, faculty members must create a system that ensures students receive additional time and support when needed.

Some schools attempt a system of interventions that has teachers stop new direct instruction and create different groups in the classroom to meet different student needs during time set aside for intervention and extension. This strategy is certainly better than traditional practice, but it is not the preferred strategy in a PLC for three reasons. First, it perpetuates the idea that a single teacher must take responsibility for a designated student group, rather than share collective responsibility for each student's learning with a teacher team. Second, it is a complex endeavor for a single teacher to simultaneously meet the needs of students requiring intervention, practice, and extension. Third, more of the same is not the best strategy for meeting student needs. A system of interventions that instead relies on the entire team or a team of intervention specialists gives students an opportunity to hear a new voice and perhaps a new strategy for learning a skill.

How Will We Extend Learning for Students Who Are Highly Proficient?

If a school focuses solely on helping students achieve their grade level or course's standards, it places an artificial ceiling on students' access to learning. For example, Adlai E. Stevenson High School in Lincolnshire, Illinois, is committed to "success for every student." It interprets that commitment as ensuring every student will graduate with high levels of learning necessary for success in college or career training. At one point in its history, the school discouraged students from learning beyond the college preparatory curriculum by establishing limits and prerequisites to serve as barriers to the advanced placement (AP) program's college-level work.

Over time, the faculty recognized that many students were capable of successfully completing college-level work while still in high school. So teachers now provide an extensive AP program and encourage all college-bound students to participate in that program while still in high school. The school also provides tutorial support for students who need assistance to succeed in the program. It has had remarkable results. Since the early 1980s, the percentage of graduating students who has successfully completed an AP course has increased from 7 percent to 90 percent, and the mode

AP exam score for students is 5, the highest possible score (Adlai E. Stevenson High School, 2017).

Every department at Stevenson also fully commits to providing highly capable students with access to academic competitions that challenge them to go beyond the traditional high school curriculum. These competitions provide both students and teachers with external benchmarks to assess the impact of the school's commitment to advancing high-performing students' learning.

Mason Crest Elementary School in Fairfax County, Virginia, is a nationally recognized Title I school that takes a different approach to extending student learning. In their planning for every unit, collaborative teams not only identify the essential standards and common formative assessments for that unit but also develop plans for extending high-performing students' learning at the end of the unit. While some team members work with students who need intervention and others work with students who need additional practice, some team members work with students who are ready for deeper exploration of the topic.

The proficiency scale approach explained in chapter 5 (page 137) provides yet another approach to addressing the issue of extending proficient students' learning. In short, a school committed to high levels of learning for all students will not establish an artificial ceiling on how much students can learn.

How Will We Increase Our Instructional Competence?

As mentioned earlier, Marzano and colleagues (2016) have added a fifth question for collaborative teams in high reliability schools to consider: How will we increase our instructional competence? This question makes sense because the high reliability school commits to ensuring more good teaching in more classrooms more of the time. Therefore, once a team has agreed on an essential standard and how it will assess student learning, members may benefit from sharing ideas about how to best teach that standard.

I fully support this idea. I also, however, must offer a caveat. The best predictor for how a teacher will teach a unit is how he or she has taught it in the past. So conversations about different practices absent evidence of student learning can easily end up discussing, "I like to teach it this way," or "I have always taught it this way." As John Hattie (2009) warns, reflective teaching has the most power when it is collective (involving a teacher team rather than an individual) and based on actual evidence of student learning.

Marzano (2009) offers similar advice when he asserts that the ultimate criterion for successful teaching is student learning, rather than any particular teacher moves. He writes, "The lesson to be learned is that educators must always look to whether a particular strategy is producing the desired results as opposed to simply assuming that if a strategy is being used, positive results will ensue" (p. 35). So although team members may benefit from a discussion about possible instructional strategies prior to teaching a unit, that discussion should never replace collective analysis of the strategies' effectiveness based on actual evidence of student learning during and after the unit.

I made the case earlier in this introduction that one of the most powerful ways a school can increase instructional competence is to have collaborative teams collectively analyze transparent results from common formative assessments. This is an important context to keep in mind when reading chapter 3.

How Will We Coordinate Our Efforts as a School?

I could not agree more with the significance of this critical question, which Marzano and colleagues (2016) have added to the HRS model of school improvement. In fact, my colleagues and I have made nondiscretionary, coordinated, schoolwide efforts a central tenet of our work. A high reliability school must address the arbitrary and capricious nature of practices that characterize too many schools and must insist that all staff honor coordinated systems and processes so that the school can strive for both excellence and equity.

It ultimately falls on school leaders to ensure the staff coordinate their collective efforts in a way that benefits students. Effective leaders can address this responsibility by establishing a simultaneously loose and tight school culture, or what Marzano and Timothy Waters (2009) have called "defined autonomy" (p. 8). Such a culture makes certain clearly understood priorities, processes, practices, and parameters are nondiscretionary. These elements of the culture are *tight* or *defined*, and effective leaders will confront those who violate or ignore the parameters. But within those few tight parameters, the culture is *loose*, which empowers individuals and teams to make decisions and enjoy a great deal of collective autonomy.

In our work with schools, my colleagues and I insist that the following three elements of the PLC process must be tight.

1. The fundamental structure of the school is the collaborative team, in which members work interdependently to achieve common goals and take collective responsibility for the learning of all students.

2. Each collaborative team does the following.

    a. Creates a guaranteed and viable curriculum, unit by unit, that provides all students with access to essential knowledge, skills, and dispositions, regardless of their assigned teacher

b. Uses an assessment process that includes frequent team-developed common formative assessments to monitor each student's learning on a timely basis

c. Applies a data-analysis protocol that uses transparent evidence of student learning to support, inform, and improve its members' individual and collective practice

3. The school creates a schoolwide plan for intervention and extension that guarantees students who experience difficulty receive additional time and support for learning in a timely, directive, coordinated, and systematic way; and that gives those who are highly proficient additional time and support to extend their learning.

An emerging theme in educational leadership finds that no one individual has the expertise, energy, and influence to bring about substantive school change. School leaders, then, must from the start face the challenge of establishing a guiding coalition or leadership team that will help guide the school through the predictable turmoil that comes with substantive cultural change. Principals should select guiding coalition members on the basis of how other faculty members respect them. They should choose the people with social capital—the people Patterson et al. (2008) refer to as *influencers* because their colleagues so trust them that if they support an idea, others will likely support it as well.

Among the guiding coalition's important tasks are the following.

- **Building the shared foundation for the PLC process:** Earlier in this introduction (page 4), I describe this task, which includes mission, vision, collective commitments, and goals. Focusing on the four pillars of mission, vision, collective commitments, and goals creates a strong foundation for the PLC process.

- **Establishing a common language so people have a shared understanding of key terms:** A principal who expects collaborative teams to develop shared norms, a guaranteed and viable curriculum, and common formative assessments will have little impact if those terms mean different things to different people throughout the faculty.

- **Building shared knowledge:** Once again, building shared knowledge together about the school's current reality and the most promising, evidence-based practices for improving it is an essential aspect of decision making in a PLC.

- **Establishing clarity about the right work:** Collaboration is morally neutral. If ambiguity arises over the work that should take place or over quality indicators regarding the work, teams will almost certainly flounder.

- **Forming systems to monitor collaborative teams' progress:** By monitoring its collaborative teams, a school can responsively help find solutions when a team struggles.

- **Creating a celebratory culture:** A celebratory culture should reinforce examples of the faculty's collective commitments and progress toward the school's shared vision.

Collaborative teams should not have sole accountability for students and their learning. Leaders should also have accountability—accountability for the teams that work with students to promote their success.

Reciprocal Accountability

Many definitions for the term *leadership* exist. My colleagues and I prefer this one: leadership is creating the conditions that allow others to succeed at what they are being asked to do (DuFour et al., 2016). This means that central office leaders, principals, and guiding coalition members must commit to reciprocal accountability. To hold teams accountable for engaging in certain processes and completing certain tasks, leaders at all levels must accept their own accountability. This way, they provide teams with the knowledge, resources, training, and ongoing support essential to their success. Effective leaders demonstrate reciprocal accountability when they do the following.

- Assign educators to meaningful teams
- Provide sufficient time to engage in meaningful collaboration
- Establish clarity regarding the work to be done and why it is important
- Monitor and support teams
- Demonstrate a willingness to confront individuals and groups who are not contributing to the collaborative team process
- Celebrate small successes along the way

Assign Educators to Meaningful Teams

We can structure educators into teams in a variety of ways. Vertical teams combine different grade levels, such as a K–2 primary team or a team of junior high and high school band directors. Interdisciplinary teams typically bring together teachers of different subjects for a particular grade level, such as seventh-grade language arts, mathematics, science, and social studies teachers. Access to technology means individuals can also link up with electronic teams, such as a team of all the art teachers in a district.

Research consistently cites that the most effective team structures for improving student achievement feature teachers of the same course or grade level, such as all the algebra teachers or second-grade teachers in a particular school (Gallimore, Ermeling, Saunders, & Goldenberg, 2009; Little, 2006; Robinson et al., 2010;

Saphier, King, & D'Auria, 2006; Stigler & Hiebert, 2009; Wei, Darling-Hammond, Andree, Richardson, & Orphanos, 2009). These structures suit the collective inquiry of collaborative teams because members share an inherent interest in addressing the six critical questions of the collaborative team process (see page 6).

Leaders who create artificial teams do damage to the PLC process. We have witnessed principals create the *leftover team*. For example, a principal may find that almost everyone on the staff fits easily into a course-specific team, but three singleton teachers—a dance instructor, an auto-repair teacher, and a band director—remain unassigned. So he or she asks those three faculty members to form a team, but it remains unclear to both the principal and the team members exactly what the three teachers should accomplish. Leaders should assign every member of a PLC to a team, but each team should serve a clear purpose—to improve student and adult learning. If the optimum team structure isn't apparent, leaders should engage teachers in a dialogue about possible team structures and get their input on which structure will most benefit them.

Provide Sufficient Time to Engage in Meaningful Collaboration

As my colleagues and I write in *Learning by Doing, Third Edition*:

> Reciprocal accountability demands that leaders who ask educators to work in collaborative teams provide those educators with time to meet during their contractual day. We believe it is insincere for any district or school leader to stress the importance of collaboration and then fail to provide time for it. One of the ways in which organizations demonstrate their priorities is allocation of resources, and in schools, one of the most precious resources is time. Thus, school and district leaders must provide teachers with time to do the things they are being asked to do. (DuFour et al., 2016, pp. 64–65)

Some school and district leaders continue to lament that they cannot find time for teachers to collaborate. No group of educators has ever *found* time to collaborate; they have to *make* time to collaborate because they consider meaningful collaboration an absolute priority. The professional literature effectively—and often—addresses the issue of finding time for collaboration, and that literature is readily available for those who have a sincere interest in exploring these alternatives. AllThingsPLC's (n.d.b) "Tools and Resources" webpage (http://bit.ly/2g9JBLJ) provides different strategies for making time for educator collaboration that do not require additional resources. Readers can go to AllThingsPLC's (n.d.a) "See the Evidence" webpage (www.all thingsplc.info/evidence) to read about hundreds of schools that have made time for educators to collaborate and have willingly shared their strategies and schedules for doing so.

These first two elements of reciprocal accountability—organizing people into meaningful teams and providing them with ample time to collaborate—are structural issues that effective school leaders can address. Other aspects of reciprocal accountability require more than managerial skill; they require leadership.

Establish Clarity Regarding the Work to Be Done and Why It Is Important

District and school leaders can support the collaborative team process in a PLC by ensuring all team members clearly understand both the nature of the work they need to do and why that work is important. Ineffective or unproductive team meetings create cynicism and only serve to sour teachers' attitudes toward teaming up while simultaneously reinforcing the norms of isolation so prevalent in our schools (Boston Consulting Group, 2014).

As my colleagues and I write in *Learning by Doing*:

> We have seen schools in which staff members are willing to collaborate about any number of things—dress codes, tardy policies, the appropriateness of Halloween parties—provided they can return to their classrooms and continue to do what they have always done. Yet in a PLC, the reason teachers are organized into teams, the reason they are provided with time to work together, the reason they are asked to focus on certain topics and complete specific tasks is so that when they return to their classrooms, they will possess and utilize an expanded repertoire of skills, strategies, materials, assessments, and ideas in order to impact student achievement in a more positive way.
>
> Therefore, one of the most important elements of reciprocal accountability that district and school leaders must address is establishing clear parameters and priorities that guide teamwork toward the goal of improved student learning. (DuFour et al., 2016, pp. 67–68)

The guiding coalition can foster this clarity by working with teams to establish a timeline for completing certain tasks in the PLC process. This work should provide the rationale behind these important tasks and examples of what quality work looks like. For example, imagine a guiding coalition created the following timeline of four activities that guides the work of collaborative teams.

1. Use our professional development days prior to the start of the school year to create and present our team norms and SMART goals before students arrive at school.

2. By the second week of school, present our list of the essential knowledge, skills, and dispositions students should acquire throughout the school year.

3. By the third week of school, administer a collaborative team–developed common formative assessment.

4. By the fourth week of school, complete our first data analysis of the evidence of student learning from our team-developed common formative assessment.

Note that each activity should result in a product that flows from a collaborative team engaged in the right work. For each product the timeline asks the team to create, the guiding coalition would present both the rationale as to why the product is critical to the team's work and high-quality examples of that product. My colleagues and I specifically designed *Learning by Doing* (DuFour et al., 2016) to provide collaborative teams with the rationale behind the different aspects of the PLC process and examples and rubrics to help guide their work. Educators can play an important role in their organization's success when they not only know how to perform specific tasks but also understand how their work contributes to a larger purpose (DuFour & Fullan, 2013).

Monitor and Support Teams

What leaders pay attention to can powerfully communicate their priorities. Leaders who simply urge teams to "go collaborate," and then have no process for monitoring the teams, send the message that they don't really find the teams' work that important. Furthermore, unless they have a process for monitoring teamwork, leaders put themselves in no position to support a struggling team or to learn from a high-performing team.

However, monitoring and micromanaging are different. Monitoring works best when teachers understand the work that teams need to produce, the expected quality of their work products, and the process for submitting work products to school leaders according to a timeline, as previously described. If a team cannot generate a product or it presents inconsistent work that lacks clearly defined quality expectations, the team needs additional support. Conversely, teams that have no difficulty producing high-quality work according to the agreed-on timeline will benefit from greater autonomy. In high-performing PLCs, collaborative teams are remarkably self-directed.

Establishing team leaders ensures the lines of communication among teams and school leaders remain open. Not only does this promote more widely dispersed leadership, it provides another avenue for school leaders to monitor the work of teams. Principals should meet with team leaders regularly; clarify and rehearse how these leaders can lead their colleagues through the different elements of the PLC process; and share problems, concerns, and successes (Eaker & Sells, 2016).

Effective team leaders can play an important role in developing their colleagues' self-efficacy. When they do, if the principal and other key staff eventually leave the school, it causes no sense of lost purpose or direction because the school has groomed many leaders who can continue to support the work.

Demonstrate a Willingness to Confront Individuals and Groups Who Are Not Contributing to the Collaborative Team Process

Perhaps the most common reason that leaders fail to effectively communicate their organization's purpose and priorities is that a disconnect appears between what they say and what they do. James A. Autry (2004), author of *The Servant Leader*, advises leaders that others in the organization:

> Can determine who you are only by observing what you do. They can't see inside your head, they can't know what you think or how you feel, they can't subliminally detect your compassion or pain or joy or goodwill. In other words, the only way you can manifest your character, your personhood, and your spirit in the workplace is through your behavior. (p. 1)

The key to effective communication lies not in the leader's eloquence but in the congruence between his or her words and deeds. Nothing destroys a leader's credibility faster than an unwillingness to address an obvious problem that stands in contrast to the organization's stated purpose and priorities. The very essence of a tight culture is the certainty that we confront any behavior inconsistent with what is tight. I have never found a tight school culture with a principal who lacks a willingness to challenge inappropriate behavior on the part of individuals or groups within the school.

Celebrate Small Successes Along the Way

Every organization will face the challenge of sustaining momentum over time while it implements a comprehensive improvement effort. Experts on the organizational change process offer consistent advice regarding that challenge: plan for frequent celebrations of incremental progress (Amabile & Kramer, 2010; Collins, 2001; Elmore & City, 2007; Heath & Heath, 2010; Katzenbach & Smith, 1993; Kotter & Cohen, 2002; Patterson et al., 2008).

When celebrations continually remind people of the purpose and priorities of their organization, team members will more likely embrace the purpose and work toward the agreed-on priorities. Regular public recognition of specific collaborative efforts, accomplished tasks, achieved goals, team learning, continuous improvement, and support for student learning remind staff of the collective commitment to create a PLC. The word *recognize* comes from the Latin for "to know again." Recognition provides opportunities to say, "Let us all be reminded of and know again what is important, what we value, and what we are committed to do. Now, let's all honor a team or individual in our school who is living that commitment."

There is a difference between *planning* for celebration and *hoping* for something to celebrate. Leaders of the PLC process identify specific benchmarks along the journey and prepare to publicly celebrate those benchmarks. In doing so, they should keep the following four guidelines for celebration in mind (DuFour et al., 2016).

1. **Explicitly state the purpose of celebration:** Continually remind staff members that celebration represents both an important strategy for reinforcing the school or district's shared mission, vision, collective commitments, and goals and the most powerful tool for sustaining the PLC journey.

2. **Make celebration everyone's responsibility:** Everyone in the organization, not just the administration, has responsibility for recognizing extraordinary commitments. Encourage all staff members to publicly report when they appreciate and admire the work of a colleague.

3. **Establish a clear link between the recognition and the behavior or commitment you are attempting to encourage and reinforce:** Recognition must specifically link to the school's or district's mission, vision, collective commitments, and goals for it to help shape the school culture. The question, What behavior or commitment have we attempted to encourage with this recognition? should have a readily apparent answer.

4. **Create opportunities to have many people recognized:** Celebration can cause disruptions and detriment if people perceive that recognition is reserved for an exclusive few. Developing a PLC requires creating systems specifically designed not only to provide celebrations but also to ensure that the celebrations recognize many winners.

Can we overdo celebration? Absolutely! We should use the sincerity with which we give recognition for a team or individual as the criterion for assessing the appropriateness of the recognition. A commendation should represent genuine and heartfelt appreciation and admiration. If it does meet that criterion, don't worry about expressing too much gratitude.

In This Book

Leaders hoping to create a high reliability school must recognize that their challenge does not merely involve putting new structures and strategies in place. They must face their larger challenge of reshaping the school culture and the assumptions, beliefs, and expectations that drive the culture. A growing consensus states that leaders can best lead this cultural transformation and create sustainable school improvement by building educators' capacity to function as members of a PLC. With a strong PLC process in place, principals and teachers put themselves in a great position to implement the other key elements of a high reliability school.

Chapter 1 provides an overview of high reliability organizations and school leadership, including the early days of school leadership and the characteristics of effective school leaders. It also presents a four-step process for creating leading indicators to establish criteria for school success. These criteria are based on the leading indicators in each level of the HRS model. In all, there are twenty-five leading indicators which form the basis for their respective lagging indicators. Chapters 2–6 cover the five levels of the HRS model: a safe, supportive, and collaborative culture; effective teaching in every classroom; a guaranteed and viable curriculum; standards-referenced reporting; and competency-based education.

More specifically, chapter 2 addresses level 1 of the HRS model—a safe, supportive, and collaborative environment. The leading indicators at this level represent critical actions and initiatives the PLC process should support to create a psychological and operational foundation for effective schooling. Chapter 3 addresses level 2—effective instruction in every classroom. The leading indicators at this level specify how the PLC process can implicitly and explicitly develop teachers to the highest levels of competence. Chapter 4 discusses level 3 of the HRS model—a guaranteed and viable curriculum. In this level, the PLC process focuses on ensuring a curriculum that is consistent from teacher to teacher and focused enough to allow for rigorous analysis of content by students. Chapter 5 covers level 4—standards-referenced reporting. Here, the PLC process ensures that the school sets appropriate goals and reports progress for individual students as well as the school as a whole. Chapter 6 addresses level 5 of the HRS model—competency-based education. Here the PLC process must help facilitate a paradigm shift that allows students to move at their pace through content. At this level, traditional approaches to scheduling and use of time are completely transformed.

Chapters 2–6 also include information on lagging indicators, quick data and continuous improvement, and leader accountability for every leading indicator. Leader accountability sections offer a proficiency scale that leaders can use to judge their effectiveness relative to the corresponding indicator.

Each chapter concludes with a section on transformations, which features significant quotes and thoughts from leaders whose schools have experienced improvement based on implementing these leading indicators. Finally, chapter 7 concludes with how district leadership can establish roles, collaborative teams, and commitments to ensure they build high reliability schools.

Leaders who hope to build and sustain high reliability schools where high levels of learning for *all* is the reality must consider the PLC process as the cornerstone of the HRS model. The remainder of this book is designed to describe the five HRS levels and explain how the PLC process brings each level to life in the real world of schools.

Chapter 1

High Reliability Organizations and School Leadership

● ● ●

Rick DuFour's introduction provides the context for schools that seek high reliability status using the PLC process as a foundation. Without a doubt, the PLC process, particularly as articulated by Rick and his colleagues, brings the vision of a true high reliability school within our grasp.

It is important to remember that the PLC process and the HRS model developed independently of one another. The PLC process has its roots in the literature on professional collaboration (Rosenholtz, 1991) as well as reflective practice (Schön, 1983; Stenhouse, 1975). The term *professional learning community* became popular in education in the 1990s (Cuban, 1992; Hord, 1997; Louis, Marks, & Kruse, 1996; McLaughlin, 1993). These early discussions noted it was the work of Rick DuFour and his colleagues that solidified the nature and importance of the PLC process in K–12 education (DuFour, DuFour, & Eaker, 2008; DuFour, DuFour, Eaker, & Many, 2010; DuFour & Eaker, 1998).

The concept of a high reliability organization (HRO) has its roots in the study of highly volatile situations. G. Thomas Bellamy and his colleagues (Bellamy, Crawford, Marshall, & Coulter, 2005) explain:

> The study of HROs has evolved through empirical investigation of catastrophic accidents, near misses, and organizations that succeed despite very trying and dangerous circumstances. Launched by Perrow's (1984) analysis of the nuclear accident at Three Mile Island, the literature evolved through discussions of whether such accidents are inevitable, as Perrow suggested, or might be avoided through

strategies used by organizations that operate successfully in high-risk conditions (Bierly & Spender, 1995; Roberts, 1990). Although there are some similarities between this literature and research on organizational effectiveness and quality improvement, HROs "have been treated as exotic outliers in mainstream organizational theory because of their unique potentials for catastrophic consequences and interactively complex technology" (Weick et al., 1999, p. 81). (p. 385)

Bellamy and his colleagues popularized the notion of applying the concept of HROs to K–12 education.

It is the confluence of these two distinct lines of theory and development that forms the basis of this book. As the title indicates, this book discusses that intersection of the PLC process and the HRS framework from the perspective of leadership.

A central tenet of this book is that effective leadership should occur within an HRO context. This would necessitate a specific process of gathering, analyzing, and interpreting certain types of data regarding what occurs in schools on a day-to-day basis. When those data indicate that something has gone awry or will soon go awry, schools must take immediate corrective action. When those data indicate that all is well, schools offer appropriate acknowledgments and celebrations. This information loop's defining feature is that it operates with extreme efficiency and attention to detail, so much so that a school might consider itself *highly reliable* as to its continuous improvement.

This approach minimizes the importance of a school leader's personal characteristics and maximizes critical, data-informed actions a leader takes. Effective leadership is not a function of having a specific personality type or a certain demeanor; it is a function of informed action aimed at continuous improvement.

Before covering the specifics of this leadership approach in depth, we find it useful to briefly summarize some past research on school leadership.

Early Days of School Leadership and Effective Schools

The importance of school leadership in a high-performing school began to emerge during the Effective Schools movement in the late 1960s and early 1970s. In 1979, Ronald Edmonds first identified effective schools' correlates in a seminal article titled "Effective Schools for the Urban Poor." At the time, his list included six variables, one of which was *strong administrative leadership*. By 1982, Edmonds whittled down the variables to the five well-known effective schools' correlates in a paper titled *Programs of School Improvement: An Overview*. In that paper, Edmonds (1982) notes that characteristics of an effective school include the following:

1. The leadership of the principal notable for substantial attention to the quality of instruction,
2. A pervasive and broadly understood instructional focus,
3. An orderly, safe climate conducive to teaching and learning,
4. Teacher behaviors that convey the expectation that all students are expected to obtain at least minimum mastery, and
5. The use of measures of pupil achievement as the basis for program evaluation. (p. 8)

Edmonds was certainly not the only researcher who recognized the importance of school leadership for student achievement during this era. Many others identified school leadership as an important variable as well, including George Weber (1971), Beverly Caffee Glenn and Taylor McLean (1981), and Wilbur B. Brookover (1979). Although a well-articulated definition of *instructional leadership* did not exist during the early days of the Effective Schools movement, effective schools researchers knew that it was a crucial ingredient. So, what goes into building effective school leaders? It turns out that they share many of the same characteristics.

Characteristics of Effective School Leaders

Since the initial work of Edmonds in 1979, the research community has continued to generate lists of effective school leaders' characteristics. Remarkably, each update to the research base seems to reach the same conclusions on which school leadership factors (albeit named and described differently) impact student learning. In other words, as the research on school leadership expands, the same variables seem to rise to the top as most influential.

Robert Marzano, Timothy Waters, and Brian McNulty (2005) completed one of the early meta-analyses on school leadership. Following this came the largest and most comprehensive study on leadership practices, which influences student achievement to date: *Investigating the Links to Improved Student Learning: Final Report of Research Findings* (Louis, Leithwood, Wahlstrom, & Anderson, 2010). The Wallace Foundation commissioned this multiyear study, and researchers from the University of Minnesota and the University of Toronto ran the study. The findings suggest four general categories of leadership functions and sixteen leadership practices that influence student achievement (Louis et al., 2010). They include:

1. Setting directions
   a. Building a shared vision
   b. Fostering the acceptance of group goals
   c. Creating high performance expectations
   d. Communicating the direction
2. Developing people

      a. Providing individualized support and consideration

      b. Offering intellectual stimulation

      c. Modeling appropriate values and practices

3. Redesigning the organization

      a. Building collaborative cultures

      b. Restructuring the organization to support collaboration

      c. Building productive relationships with families and communities

      d. Connecting the school to the wider community

4. Managing the instructional program

      a. Staffing the program

      b. Providing instructional support

      c. Monitoring school activity

      d. Buffering staff from distractions to their work

      e. Aligning resources

In 2016, Dallas Hambrick Hitt and Pamela D. Tucker (2016) synthesized the research on leadership characteristics that impact student learning. Unlike some school leadership syntheses, Hitt and Tucker's (2016) synthesis focuses only on peer-reviewed, empirical research. They identify three broad leadership frameworks that meet their criteria for inclusion and combine them into a new blended framework. The three frameworks are the Orlando Leadership Framework, the Learning Centered Leadership Framework, and the Essential Supports Framework. Through their synthesis, Hitt and Tucker (2016) have generated the following five domains that impact student achievement:

1. Establishing and conveying the vision
2. Facilitating a high-quality learning experience for students
3. Building professional capacity
4. Creating a supportive organization for learning
5. Connecting with external partners (p. 542)

In addition, they identify twenty-eight practices embedded in the five domains. These five domains and twenty-eight leadership practices further demonstrate the similarities in multiple researchers' findings over many years (Brookover & Lezotte, 1979; Cotton, 2003; Deal & Kennedy, 1983; Donmoyer, 1985; Duke, 1982; Elmore, 2003; Fullan, 2001; Heifetz, 1994; Heifetz & Laurie, 2001; Leithwood, 1994; Sergiovanni, 2004; Youngs & King, 2002).

As mentioned previously, one striking thing about the history of research on school leadership is its relative consistency. One might say that as a profession, educators have developed a robust understanding of leadership factors in the research literature. Unfortunately, this enhanced knowledge has not turned into a coherent theory of action that enhances student achievement. We believe that to turn what we know about leadership into actionable knowledge, one must take a high reliability perspective.

A High Reliability Perspective

The concept of high reliability organizations has come up in the general literature for quite some time. For example, in the mid-1980s, the University of California, Berkeley launched a project known as the High Reliability Organizations Project. The Berkeley group set out to study high-hazard organizations that avoided failures and maintained success over time better than their peers in the same industries. In a paper titled *The Legacy of the Theory of High Reliability Organizations: An Ethnographic Endeavor*, Mathilde Bourrier (2011), among a number of inferences, concludes that high reliability organizations have a laser focus on using data to make decisions that themselves focus on continuous improvement. Another critical characteristic of high reliability organizations is awareness of the highly interdependent systems that characterize the daily operations of the organization. Bourrier (2011) states:

> The HRS literature substantiated that safety and reliability are not only the result of great technology in combination with great culture. They are also the result of organization design: choices and allocations are made which greatly influence the potential to be safe and reliable. These decisions have to be questioned and reflected upon constantly. (p. 4)

Karl E. Weick and Kathleen M. Sutcliffe (2007) report similar findings from analyzing the literature on high reliability organizations.

While the initial literature and research on high reliability organizations focused on high-hazard industries, the concept of high reliability organizations has continued to evolve and now has visibility in the literature of professional industries such as health care, oil and gas, transportation, and international commerce. In 2014, worldwide consulting group North Highland produced a paper on the concept, reporting that "organizations that conduct consistent, sustainable, and low-error operations [are] based on informed, high-quality decision making and controls" (p. 2). North Highland (2014) identifies five aspects of operation that a high reliability organization practices:

- Organize its efforts to increase the amount and quality of attention to failure and data analysis.
- Engage every member and level of the organization in the problem-resolution and prevention process.

- Increase alertness to detail so all people can detect subtle differences in context by examining data and looking for predictions.
- Focus on what the organization needs to do to reach the performance target on a continuous basis.
- Act as a 'mindful' organization; thinking and learning constantly by empowering individuals to interact continuously with others in the organization as they develop in their roles. (p. 3)

Although several examples of high reliability organizations appear in various industries, schools have not typically operated as such. However, some educators have called for schools to begin taking a high reliability perspective. Sam Stringfield (1995) first made the case, indicating that schools should use high reliability implementation methods for school reform. Sam Stringfield and Amanda Datnow (2002) maintain that any school-based reform should increase reliability through the use of high reliability strategies. Since 1995, the pressure for schools to begin taking a high reliability perspective has continued to mount. As G. Thomas Bellamy, Lindy Crawford, Laura Huber Marshall, and Gail A. Coulter (2005) state:

> The stakes for failure have been raised so high—both for schools and for students— that *high reliability* has become an important aspect of school success. Schools are now challenged to prevent practically all failures and to close achievement gaps among student groups—in short, to ensure highly reliable learning for all students. (p. 384)

This pressure has grown with the Every Student Succeeds Act (ESSA), which, according to the U.S. Department of Education (2017), "requires—for the first time—that all students in America be taught to high academic standards that will prepare them to succeed in college and careers." Ensuring that *all* students learn at high levels requires schools and their staff to take a high reliability perspective.

In their analyses of high reliability organizations, Bellamy et al. (2005) identify three functions related to high reliability:

1. Improving normal operations
2. Detecting potential problems
3. Recovering from those problems (p. 390)

These three functions serve as the foundation of their fail-safe schools framework. The HRS model builds on this work with its leading and lagging indicators.

Leading and Lagging Indicators

At its core, a high reliability perspective involves monitoring the relationship between actions an organization takes to enhance its effectiveness and the extent to which these actions do, in fact, produce the desired effects. The literature on high reliability organizations refers to what an organization does to ensure it succeeds as *leading indicators*, and it refers to the concrete results produced from monitoring the effects of the leading indicators as *lagging indicators*. Leading and lagging indicators are the operational cornerstones of the high reliability organization process.

From this perspective, most research literature on school leadership tends to state research findings in terms of leading indicators. To illustrate, consider the five variables Edmonds originally identified. Stating that effective leaders should foster a "pervasive and broadly understood instructional focus" certainly provides direction and even implies specific actions, but it does not provide much clarity as to the desired effects of such actions (Edmonds, 1982, p. 8). The Wallace Foundation also mostly phrases the variables it offers as leading indicators (see page 25). "Building a shared vision," for example, implies specific actions leaders can take (Louis et al., 2010). But leaders cannot monitor how people follow this mandate to build a vision without clearly articulated outcomes. Likewise, "offering intellectual stimulation" implies specific actions; but without a description of intended outcomes, such actions are difficult to monitor (Louis et al., 2010).

We do not intend to demean the previous efforts to describe effective leadership. Indeed, leading indicators provide specific guidance on possible actions and interventions that can occur in a school. Lagging indicators complement such actions by articulating desired effects in concrete terms.

To a great extent, then, schools wishing to become HRSs must translate the research literature's recommended actions into those actions' desired effects. This is the essence of lagging indicators. To illustrate, consider the following leading indicator from the Wallace Foundation study: "building a shared vision" (Louis et al., 2010). Although this certainly seems like an intuitively obvious action a school should engage in, translating this into a corresponding lagging indicator involves articulating that shared vision's desired effect or effects. For example, the lagging indicator could say this: "Staff members perceive that they are part of a concerted effort to improve the lives of the school's students."

Lagging indicators prove most useful when they describe concrete or quantitative evidence that the school's actions have produced specific desired effects. For example, this lagging indicator for the leading indicator of building a shared vision contains a more concrete description: "A survey indicates that at least 85 percent of the staff perceive they are part of a concerted effort to improve the lives of the school's students." Consequently, we define *lagging indicators* as concrete and, in some cases, quantifiable outcomes for which schools can establish minimum acceptable criteria.

So, where does one start in implementing the leading indicators that build a high reliability school? It begins with doing the right work.

The Right Work

To start building an HRS, a school must identify leading indicators critical to the school's success. This is foundational to what Elmore (2003) refers to as "doing the right work." He contends that doing the right work is the primary factor in school improvement. He further notes that in the United States, a perception persists that "schools fail because the people in them—administrators, teachers, and students—don't work hard enough; and that they are lazy, unmotivated, and self-serving" (Elmore, 2003, p. 9). However, the truth of the matter is that hard-working, highly motivated administrators, teachers, and students frequently populate failing schools. They do not have a problem with *working hard*; their problem lies in selecting the *right work*.

In this book, we offer twenty-five leading indicators that we believe represent the right work in schools. Chapters 2–6 cover these leading indicators in depth. We draw this list of leading indicators directly from previously cited research that we have vetted over a number of years (Carbaugh, Marzano, & Toth, 2015; Marzano, 2001, 2003; Marzano & Waters, 2009; Marzano, Waters, & McNulty, 2005).

Specifically, we can trace our HRS model back to school effectiveness work done at the turn of the 21st century (for a full, detailed discussion of the research supporting this model, see Marzano, in press). We have also vetted this model in the context of principal evaluation (Carbaugh, Marzano, & Toth, 2015; Herman et al., 2016; Marzano, Waters, & McNulty, 2005). Finally, this model contains many of the highest-ranking variables from Hattie's 195 variables related to achievement (see Hattie, 2009, 2012, 2015).

Table 1.1 presents the twenty-five leading indicators in the HRS model, organized into five levels. This hierarchical structure has some intuitive appeal.

Table 1.1: HRS Model

Level	Leading Indicators
Level 1: Safe, Supportive, and Collaborative Culture	1.1—The faculty and staff perceive the school environment as safe, supportive, and orderly.
	1.2—Students, parents, and the community perceive the school environment as safe, supportive, and orderly.
	1.3—Teachers have formal roles in the decision-making process regarding school initiatives.
	1.4—Collaborative teams regularly interact to address common issues regarding curriculum, assessment, instruction, and the achievement of all students.
	1.5—Teachers and staff have formal ways to provide input regarding the optimal functioning of the school.
	1.6—Students, parents, and the community have formal ways to provide input regarding the optimal functioning of the school.
	1.7—The school acknowledges the success of the whole school as well as individuals within the school.
	1.8—The school manages its fiscal, operational, and technological resources in a way that directly supports teachers.
Level 2: Effective Teaching in Every Classroom	2.1—The school communicates a clear vision as to how teachers should address instruction.
	2.2—The school supports teachers to continually enhance their pedagogical skills through reflection and professional growth plans.
	2.3—The school is aware of and monitors predominant instructional practices.
	2.4—The school provides teachers with clear, ongoing evaluations of their pedagogical strengths and weaknesses that are based on multiple sources of data and are consistent with student achievement data.
	2.5—The school provides teachers with job-embedded professional development that is directly related to their instructional growth goals.
	2.6—Teachers have opportunities to observe and discuss effective teaching.
Level 3: Guaranteed and Viable Curriculum	3.1—The school curriculum and accompanying assessments adhere to state and district standards.
	3.2—The school curriculum is focused enough that teachers can adequately address it in the time they have available.
	3.3—All students have the opportunity to learn the critical content of the curriculum.
	3.4—The school establishes clear and measurable goals that are focused on critical needs regarding improving overall student achievement at the school level.
	3.5—The school analyzes, interprets, and uses data to regularly monitor progress toward school achievement goals.
	3.6—The school establishes appropriate school- and classroom-level programs and practices to help students meet individual achievement goals when data indicate interventions are needed.

continued →

Level	Leading Indicators
Level 4: Standards-Referenced Reporting	4.1—The school establishes clear and measurable goals focused on critical needs regarding improving achievement of individual students. 4.2—The school analyzes, interprets, and uses data to regularly monitor progress toward achievement goals for individual students.
Level 5: Competency-Based Education	5.1—Students move on to the next level of the curriculum for any subject area only after they have demonstrated competence at the previous level. 5.2—The school schedule accommodates students moving at a pace appropriate to their situation and needs. 5.3—The school affords students who have demonstrated competency levels greater than those articulated in the system immediate opportunities to begin work on advanced content or career paths of interest.

Level 1 of the HRS hierarchy is foundational because it addresses foundational human needs. If students, teachers, and parents do not perceive the school as safe, supportive, and collaborative, they will focus their attention on getting these needs met, as opposed to on the content addressed in school.

Level 2 deals with effective teaching. It appears second in the hierarchy because it is one of the hierarchy's most influential and alterable variables. Research has consistently supported the notion that the quality of teaching a student receives has a profound effect on his or her academic achievement (Nye, Konstantopoulos, & Hedges, 2004). Additionally, deliberate practice can enhance teachers' pedagogical skill (Ericsson & Charness, 1994; Ericsson, Krampe, & Tesch-Romer, 1993).

Level 3 deals with a curriculum that is both guaranteed and viable. *Guaranteed* means that no matter who teaches a given course or grade level, students in that course or grade will receive the same content. *Viable* means that the content has enough focus that teachers have adequate time and resources to teach it. Some educators have asked why a guaranteed and viable curriculum does not appear second in the hierarchy. Placing a guaranteed and viable curriculum before teaching would imply that it is more important to student learning than teaching. However, we assert that an effective teacher can overcome a weak curriculum, whereas a strong curriculum cannot overcome a weak teacher.

The first three levels of the hierarchy represent work in which all schools must engage at all times. Culture, teaching, and curriculum are the bedrocks of schooling. Then, levels 4 and 5 in the hierarchy represent systems change. Level 4 identifies a form of recordkeeping and reporting that allows schools to monitor individual students' status and growth in specific topics. This represents a major shift in the way a school is run. Level 5 goes even further. It not only allows educators to monitor individual students but also allows students to move through the curriculum at their own pace.

Once a school has established the right work, it can follow four steps that lead to HRS status. As we discuss in subsequent chapters, these four steps become integrated into the PLC process. For a particular indicator, one collaborative team might take the lead for some or all steps. For another indicator, all collaborative teams might share equal responsibility.

The Four Steps

We have developed the following four steps in our work with more than six hundred schools relative to the HRS process. In effect, if a school engages in the actions described in these steps, it will attain high reliability status, leading indicator by leading indicator.

The four steps include:

1. Create lagging indicators and establish criteria for success.
2. Collect data on school status regarding lagging indicators.
3. If the school hasn't met lagging indicator minimum requirements, refocus on actions inherent in associated leading indicators.
4. Continually collect data on lagging indicators and respond accordingly.

Create Lagging Indicators and Establish Criteria for Success

If a school uses the HRS model as described in this book, by definition, it will already have its leading indicators at all five levels. As described previously, a lagging indicator translates a leading indicator into observable results or products. To illustrate, consider leading indicator 1.4: "Collaborative teams regularly interact to address common issues regarding curriculum, assessment, instruction, and the achievement of all students." Of course, a school should already have initiated the PLC process and, as a result, have collaborative teams in place. In effect, for PLC schools, this leading indicator (and others) is automatically addressed.

To translate this into a lagging indicator, school leaders would have to identify what they would observe if the PLC process worked well. For example, as part of a lagging indicator, school leaders might note that teams should meet a specific number of times throughout the month. They can observe and quantify such behavior. School leaders might also note that teams should submit summary notes for all meetings that articulate the issues addressed in the meeting and the action items identified as a result of the team's deliberations. Leaders might articulate the lagging indicator as follows: "Collaborative teams meet each week about specific teaching and learning issues and submit team-developed products (for example, lists of essential standards, common pacing guides, team-developed common assessments, analyses of data from common assessments) and the actions teams decide to take."

Finally, school leaders should establish a criterion for success so they can determine whether the desired behaviors identified in the lagging indicator, in fact, occur. For this lagging indicator, they might add the following sentence: "All teams must submit their products and action plans after each meeting, and the leadership team must review and provide feedback on the quality of the products and the clarity of the actions teams identify."

Collect Data on School Status Regarding Lagging Indicators

When leaders have well-designed and articulated lagging indicators in place, they should find it easy to collect relevant data. In the case of indicator 1.4, school leaders would simply collect the products and action steps submitted by collaborative teams and analyze them for quality.

Sometimes, lagging indicators point the leadership team to perceptual data. To illustrate, consider leading indicator 1.1: "The faculty and staff perceive the school environment as safe, supportive, and orderly." The lagging indicator associated with it might say this: "At least 90 percent of faculty and staff perceive the school to be safe, supportive, and orderly." To evaluate the school relative to this lagging indicator, a questionnaire would have to be developed and administered to faculty and staff. Questionnaires would involve a series of questions or statements such as the following:

- Our school is a safe place.
- Our school is supportive.
- Our school is an orderly place.
- We know the emergency procedures for our school.

The faculty and staff would respond to these statements using a scale such as: strongly disagree, disagree, neither disagree nor agree, agree, or strongly agree. (For examples of survey items, see Marzano, Warrick, & Simms, 2014). In some cases, data for lagging indicators can include concrete products, such as a written language of instruction for leading indicator 2.1.

If the School Hasn't Met Lagging Indicator Minimum Requirements, Refocus on Actions Inherent in Associated Leading Indicators

This step implies that leaders establish some type of school certification. By this, we mean that the data the school leaders collect for a lagging indicator show that the school has met the criterion for that indicator. For indicator 1.4, if the leadership team considers 80 percent of collaborative teams' submitted products acceptable in terms of the importance of the issues, quality, and clarity of the actions, then leaders could legitimately conclude that they have met the criterion for 1.4. For indicator

1.1, if 90 percent of respondents indicate they consider the school a safe, supportive, and orderly place, leaders could conclude that they have met the criterion. In effect, the school can consider itself certified for this particular indicator.

On the other hand, if data indicate that teams have not met a criterion, then leaders must take action to improve performance on the indicator. For 1.4, leaders might meet with those collaborative teams that have turned in ineffective products after their meetings and help clarify expectations and provide resources, support, and training to assist teams in being successful in the right work. For 1.1, leaders might seek to identify what has occurred or has not occurred to produce the desired perception of the school's safety, supportiveness, and orderliness. We address this for each indicator in subsequent chapters. Briefly, school leaders would attempt to find out why a lagging indicator has not been met. If teams have not met the criteria for lagging indicators, leaders must take immediate action to provide what is missing to satisfy the criteria.

Continually Collect Data on Lagging Indicators and Respond Accordingly

By definition, if a school has met all lagging indicators for a specific level, it can consider itself as operating with high reliability relative to that level. Once a school has done so relative to a particular level in the HRS model, it should still collect data periodically. We refer to such data as *quick data*. As the name implies, quick data do not take much time or energy to collect, and they provide ongoing evidence as to the school's functioning on a given level. To illustrate, for indicator 1.4, leaders might continue to collect meeting products but analyze only a random sample on a systematic basis. For indicator 1.1, leaders might periodically and informally assemble teacher and staff focus groups to discuss their perceptions of safety, support, and orderliness offered by the school.

As noted previously, chapters 2–6 in this book address all four steps for levels 1–5 of the HRS model. For each leading indicator at each level, we describe:

1. Examples of lagging indicators (step 1)
2. The data school leaders should collect to validate their school's performance on the lagging indicators (step 2)
3. The actions school leaders should take when the data for a lagging indicator indicate that improvement is needed (step 3)
4. The manner in which school leaders can continually monitor their school's status on lagging indicators, even after they have validated its effectiveness (step 4)

In chapter 2, we'll discuss level 1 of the HRS model: a safe, supportive, and collaborative culture.

Chapter 2

Safe, Supportive,
and Collaborative Culture

● ● ●

In the introduction to this book, Rick explained that a collaborative culture is one of the three big ideas underlying the PLC process. He further explained that collaborative teams whose members take collective responsibility for the learning of all students must be "tight" if the PLC process is to flourish. These are some obvious reasons why level 1 of the HRS model focuses on culture.

One might describe an organization's culture as the shared beliefs of the individuals who populate the organization and the shared social behaviors and norms those individuals adhere to. Shared beliefs form the basis for most decisions made in an organization. If administrators, teachers, and staff all believe that schools should function to enhance the lives of all students, then they will make decisions about resources, programs, and policies in a manner consistent with that belief. Shared social behaviors and norms are de facto rules of conduct that people tend to conform to whether those behaviors and norms are implicit or explicit. For example, if a school accepts the social behavior that students refer to teachers by their first names, then, over time, people tend to gravitate to this convention.

A high reliability school does not leave the culture up to chance or happenstance. Rather, leaders in an HRS strive to ensure the organization fosters shared beliefs, behaviors, and norms relative to at least three areas: (1) safety, (2) support, and (3) collaboration. Although they might also include other areas, these three are essential areas of focus and concern. Of the three, collaboration serves as the keystone. Collaboration fostered by the PLC process works as the engine of level 1 in the HRS model. Indeed, it can serve as the vehicle for effectively using leading and lagging indicators, not just at level 1 but at all levels.

When educators meet and work in high-performing collaborative teams, everything else seems to run more smoothly. In fact, we believe that the PLC process is the heart of what researchers refer to as *collective efficacy* (Goddard, Hoy, & Hoy, 2004). In his 2015 synthesis of the combined findings of more than 65,000 studies, Hattie finds that teachers' collective efficacy is the second-highest-ranking variable of 195 relative to its positive impact on student learning.

Level 1 of the HRS model has eight leading indicators.

1.1 The faculty and staff perceive the school environment as safe, supportive, and orderly.

1.2 Students, parents, and the community perceive the school environment as safe, supportive, and orderly.

1.3 Teachers have formal roles in the decision-making process regarding school initiatives.

1.4 Collaborative teams regularly interact to address common issues regarding curriculum, assessment, instruction, and the achievement of all students.

1.5 Teachers and staff have formal ways to provide input regarding the optimal functioning of the school.

1.6 Students, parents, and the community have formal ways to provide input regarding the optimal functioning of the school.

1.7 The school acknowledges the success of the whole school as well as individuals within the school.

1.8 The school manages its fiscal, operational, and technological resources in a way that directly supports teachers.

Leading Indicator 1.1

The faculty and staff perceive the school environment as safe, supportive, and orderly.

Relative to leading indicator 1.1, leaders must achieve the key task of establishing schoolwide routines and procedures. In effect, safety is a byproduct of effective procedures and routines. Although that sounds obvious, leaders often take for granted that routines and procedures get clearly communicated, understood, and monitored with consistency across the entire school.

Meaningful actions school leaders might take for this indicator include creating routines and procedures focused on specific areas of the school and recommitting to established routines and procedures that are not known or observed with consistency schoolwide. The leadership team at C. D. Folkes Middle School in Round Rock, Texas, implemented this strategy when they established their schoolwide norms for students during passing time in the hallways. As part of this process, they established schoolwide norms for staff to monitor and reinforce as they supervised their assigned areas during passing periods. Norms were stated on the sheet that indicated which teachers had supervision duty in each hallway and each stairway in the school.

Some schools implement programs that we can generally categorize as *positive behavior programs*. Many aspects of these types of programs provide excellent strategies to strongly support this leading indicator. Figure 2.1 (page 40), figure 2.2 (page 41), and figure 2.3 (page 42) depict some concrete products that result from specific actions and procedures regarding this leading indicator.

The discipline matrix in figure 2.1 is our adaptation of what we have observed in the field. Matrices like these are designed to bring consistency to how teachers and administrators address and enforce student discipline across campus. It describes three types of behaviors. Type A behaviors are those teachers address in the classroom. Type B behaviors are those teachers both address and document in the classroom. Type C behaviors result in automatic referrals. Notice some behaviors are considered severe enough that they start as type B and require documentation (see empty cells in column 1). Also note that each behavior is coded as relating to one of three areas of personal responsibility: citizenship, integrity, and achievement. Prior to creating posters for figure 2.1, teachers and students should discuss the meaning of each category of personal responsibility.

Figure 2.2 depicts a poster for display in hallways, bus-loading areas, classrooms, and other areas where students can view it as a reminder of appropriate behavior and the signals from teachers that cue students to execute specific behavioral responses. Figure 2.3 depicts a student behavior tracking matrix that teachers monitor on a daily basis. The matrices include positive and negative behaviors so a teacher can use them to reinforce positive behaviors or address negative behaviors. Students are referred to as *scholars* to reinforce the fact that their daily purpose is to learn and that the staff believes they are capable of being scholars. Each scholar is expected to have his or her card every day. At the end of the week, teachers send the cards home with students so parents can have an ongoing update on their child's behavior. When a new week begins, each scholar gets a new card. This practice was very purposeful when it was implemented under the leadership of principal Trana Allen and her staff at Anderson Mill Elementary School in the Round Rock, Texas, school district.

Type A Behaviors (Typically Get Addressed in the Classroom)	Type B Behaviors (Receive a Teacher-Assigned Consequence With Documentation)	Type C Behaviors (Receive an Automatic Referral)	CIA (Citizenship, Integrity, or Achievement)
	Persistent type A behavior	Persistent type B behavior	Citizenship
	Inappropriate or offensive language (conversational cursing or such language about race, culture, sexual orientation, intelligence, and so on)	Racial, sexual, or cultural harassment (verbal or physical)	Citizenship
Inattention (sleeping, failure to stay on task, note writing, and so on)	Disrespect to an adult (back talk, comments under one's breath, or bad gestures)	Severe disrespect to an adult (cursing at a teacher, personal verbal attacks, and so on)	Integrity
Irresponsibility (failure to turn in homework or assignments, unpreparedness for class, or dishonesty)	Participation in cheating (copied homework, daily work, projects, or tests; plagiarism; or forgery)		Achievement
Chair violations (getting out of one's seat, tipping a chair, putting one's feet on a desk, and so on)	Area violations (going down the wrong hallway, using the wrong bathroom, using the stairs, misuse of a hall pass, and so on)	Skipping class or leaving campus	Achievement
Mild disruptions (talking without permission, blurting out, making noises, passing notes, and so on)	Continual, deliberate disruption of class	Serious violations of safety rules (pulling the fire alarm, calling 911, messing with hazardous materials, fighting with food, or doing malicious pranks)	Citizenship
Noncompliance with classroom or school expectations, procedures, or routines	Refusal to comply with an adult directive	Refusal to comply when safety is concerned	Citizenship
Bickering and disagreements between students	Persistent or heated conflict or provocation between students that could lead to violence	Physical violence (hitting, kicking, biting, throwing dangerous items, and so on)	Citizenship
Mild horseplay (aggravating or annoying peers, running around, or touching another student's belongings)	Moderate horseplay (possible safety issue— running, tripping, pushing, slapping, or doing pranks)	Possession of a weapon or an illegal substance	Integrity

	Moderate bullying (name calling, insults, rumor spreading, or exclusionary jokes)	Severe bullying (threats or intimidation)	Citizenship
Gossiping			
Minor bad behaviors (invasion of space, misuse of supplies, and so on)	Throwing of non-dangerous items (spit wads, pen caps, balls, and so on)	Terroristic threats	Citizenship
Use of a non-string backpack	Minor property damage	Vandalism (graffiti, damage of property, or destruction of property)	Integrity
	Minor PDA (hugging, hand holding, or close contact)	Vulgarity, obscenity, or pornography (such as kissing or major PDA)	Integrity
	Misuse of computer privileges (unauthorized use of email, games, painting tools, music, or videos)	Theft	Integrity
	Inappropriate use of a device (inappropriate material)	Distribution or sale of prohibited items	Citizenship

Source: Marzano, 2017.

Figure 2.1: Discipline matrix.

What You See	What It Means	What You Do
	Attention!	Stop talking, raise your hand, and listen to the adult.
	You committed a foul against another person, or you were not being nice or respectful.	If you committed the foul, give two put-ups (the opposite of put-downs) to the person you fouled.
	Check your behavior!	Change your behavior to follow the essential agreements.

Source: © 2018 by Anderson Mill Elementary School. Used with permission.

Figure 2.2: Behavior poster.

Behavior Report

Scholar: _____   Teacher: _____   Date: _____

Monday		Tuesday		Wednesday		Thursday		Friday	
Positive	Negative	Positive	Negative	Positive	Negative	Positive	Negative	Positive	Negative
Parent initials: ____		Parent initials: ____		Parent initials: ____		Parent initials: ____		Parent initials: ____	

Positive

1. Ready to learn (listo para aprender)
2. Responsible (responsable)
3. Respectful (respetuoso)
4. Communicator (comunicador)
5. Risk-taker (valiente)

Negative

6. Off task (fuera de tarea)
7. Unprepared (no está preparado)
8. Disrespectful (irrespetuoso)
9. Disrupting learning (interrumpiendo el aprendizaje)
10. Unsafe (inseguro)

Source: © 2018 by Anderson Mill Elementary School.

Figure 2.3: Student behavior tracking matrix.

Supportiveness is another critical aspect of leading indicator 1.1. One might think of support as a level up on the hierarchy of human needs. Robert Marzano, Darrell Scott, Tina Boogren, and Ming Lee Newcomb (2017) note that all students continually seek to have their needs met in the classroom. Indeed, human beings continually seek to have their needs met in virtually every situation they find themselves in. According to Maslow (1943, 1954), needs like physical safety and physical comfort appear at the base of the hierarchy of needs. Maslow's hierarchy, as explained by Marzano, Scott, and colleagues (2017), is shown in figure 2.4.

At the higher end appear needs like self-actualization and connection to something greater than oneself. In the middle of the hierarchy appear needs like belonging and esteem within a community of peers.

In leading indicator 1.1, *safety* certainly refers to the lower end of the hierarchy—physical comfort and physical safety. However, the term *support* in indicator 1.1 refers to the levels previously listed, starting with belonging and moving up through esteem, self-actualization, and connection to something greater than oneself.

As previously described, the school's focus on establishing order through clear and well-executed routines typically addresses directly or indirectly student needs for physical comfort and physical safety, but such routines might not suffice for student needs involving belonging and esteem. To this end, some schools design and execute specific programs and practices such as the invitational education framework (Purkey, 1991; Purkey & Novak, 1988, 1996).

The invitational framework has two dimensions: (1) invitation and (2) intention. *Invitation* refers to the extent to which the environments of individual classrooms and the school as a whole contribute to or take away from a student's sense of inclusion. *Intention* refers to the extent to which specific aspects of the environments of individual classrooms and the school as a whole are intentionally designed into the system or are simply unintended consequences of programs or practices that exist in the school. Thus, specific aspects of individual classrooms and the school as a whole can be intentionally inviting, unintentionally inviting, intentionally disinviting, or unintentionally disinviting.

With this framework in mind, teachers can ask students to identify elements they consider inviting and elements they consider disinviting. Figure 2.5 (page 44) shows a sample list.

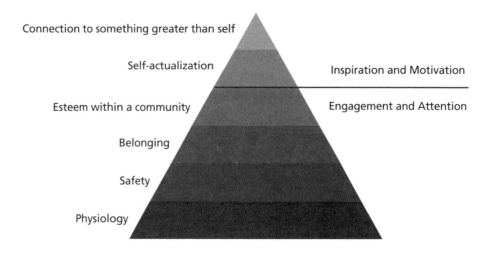

Source: Marzano, Scott, Boogren, & Newcomb, 2017, p. 5.

Figure 2.4: Maslow's hierarchy of needs.

Inviting	Disinviting
• Talking about the weekend at the start of class on Monday • Students being able to select partners for some assignments • The teacher bringing in treats as a surprise • The teacher asking students what they thought about a unit and ways it could be improved	• The teacher chewing gum while students can't • Students not being allowed into the classroom until the first bell rings • The teacher taking a long time to give feedback on assignments to students • Not having decorations in the classroom

Source: Marzano, Scott, et al., 2017, p. 97.

Figure 2.5: Inviting and disinviting classroom elements.

Once teachers and school leaders have collected such data on inviting and dis-inviting elements, they can use them to determine actions to take to enhance the classroom or school culture.

To address student needs for self-actualization and connection to something greater than oneself (the highest levels of human needs), schools typically implement programs and practices that do not show up in the traditional academic curriculum. Relative to self-actualization, some schools employ personal projects. Marzano, Scott, et al. (2017) explain that students should participate in personal projects every year, implementing the following seven steps:

1. **Identify a goal:** What do I want to accomplish?
2. **Identify mentors and role models:** Who else has accomplished this goal? Who will support me?

3. **Research the necessary experiences and skills:** What skills and resources will I need to accomplish my goal?
4. **Engage in behavior analysis:** What will I have to change [about myself] in order to achieve my goal?
5. **Create short-term and long-term plans:** What is my plan for achieving my goal?
6. **Take small steps:** What small steps can I take right now?
7. **Reflect on the process:** How have I been doing? What have I learned about myself? (p. 56)

As the steps illustrate, participation in personal projects allows students to work on personally meaningful and, consequently, intrinsically motivating goals. Allowing students to work on projects like this helps generate their perceptions that the school is interested in them as individuals.

Lagging Indicators

In chapter 1, we described four steps that guide leaders through the actions they must take to operate as a high reliability school. Steps 1, 2, and 3 (see page 35) all focus on the design and initial use of lagging indicators. Step 1 involves creating lagging indicators, step 2 involves collecting data regarding the school's status on lagging indicators, and step 3 involves either verifying that the school does well on lagging indicators or putting more energy into enhancing performance on lagging indicators. To see how this might play out, consider the following example.

Break-O-Day Elementary School in New Whiteland, Indiana, developed a lagging indicator for leading indicator 1.1 to decrease the number of student office referrals per month by 50 percent (from twenty referrals to ten referrals) because office referrals cut into precious class time. To decrease the number of referrals, members of the school leadership team concluded that they needed to understand why students received the referrals in the first place. They dug into available data and found some common reasons that students received referrals, especially during recess. To address these issues, staff made videos depicting appropriate behavior and inappropriate behavior at recess. They aimed to reduce referrals by teaching students about useful versus disruptive ways to behave, use equipment, and interact with one another. To see if the approach worked, the school collected data by logging all office referrals on a daily basis. At the end of each month, the school's guiding coalition pulled together the data, reviewed the data, and discussed whether these data met the criterion scores for the lagging indicators they had established. They also discussed whether they could publically celebrate the data or whether they needed to utilize additional strategies to bring down the office referral numbers.

Other lagging indicators that address leading indicator 1.1 include:

- Climate survey data indicate that 95 percent of faculty and staff claim they consider the school a safe, supportive, and orderly place.

- Posters across the school communicate specific rules and procedures expected within the school.

- Data show less than 5 percent of the student body are getting removed from class or school for unsafe or disorderly conduct.

- School leaders provide evidence of practicing emergency management procedures for specific incidents.

Quick Data and Continuous Improvement

Step 4 of the HRS process indicates that once a school has demonstrated it meets the identified criterion relative to a specific leading indicator, it must continue to collect data and act on inferences drawn from those data. This does not mean that a school must collect data for every lagging indicator for all levels every week or even every month. Instead, once school leaders have certified their school meets the criterion for a lagging indicator (for example, they have indicated they've met the criterion in their lagging indicator), they should periodically (for example, once per month) collect quick data on a rotating basis. For example, they collect data for one lagging indicator one month and then collect data for another lagging indicator the next month.

It is important to remember that, as the name implies, quick data don't take long to gather. They can come from observations and brief informal conversations. Given the flexibility of quick data, school leaders can quite easily gather them on multiple lagging indicators during a single observation or discussion. Also, quick data might already reside within reports the school receives from the district or other sources it regularly receives. Finally, remember that administrators should react to the quick data they receive. Many times, this reaction means acknowledging or celebrating that things are going well. In other cases, quick data might indicate that leaders must attend to a given lagging indicator because it appears that performance in this area has declined. The more quickly a school works to solve a problem or potential problem elucidated by quick data, the more effectively it operates as an HRS. This dynamic is the heart of the continuous improvement process.

Other examples of quick data sources include the following.

- Counselors review monthly discipline data to monitor trends by time of day and time of year.

- Custodians share what they see regarding if students follow the rules for passing in the halls during passing periods.

- Administrators periodically observe staff to make sure they stand at their assigned duty stations for student supervision during passing time.

Leader Accountability

Fundamentally, this book is about leading high reliability schools. By definition, this means the book is also about leaders having accountability for a school's status on each leading indicator. To this end, we offer performance scales for each leading indicator in the HRS model. Figure 2.6 depicts the scale for leading indicator 1.1. Our recommendation is that school leaders continuously rate themselves using the scales we have provided. Scores of "developing" or below indicate that there is still work to be done if teachers desire their schools to operate as high reliability organizations.

Sustaining	Applying	Developing	Beginning	Not Attempting
The school continually cultivates information through quick data sources to monitor faculty and staff perceptions of the safety, supportiveness, and orderliness of the school environment, and it takes proper actions to intervene when quick data indicate a potential problem.	The school has developed and implemented well-defined, schoolwide routines and procedures that lead to faculty and staff perceptions of a safe, supportive, and orderly environment, and it can produce lagging indicators to show the desired effects of these actions.	The school has developed and implemented well-defined, schoolwide routines and procedures that lead to faculty and staff perceptions of a safe, supportive, and orderly environment.	The school is in the beginning, yet incomplete, stages of developing and implementing well-defined, schoolwide routines and procedures that lead to faculty and staff perceptions of a safe, supportive, and orderly environment.	The school has not attempted to develop and implement well-defined, schoolwide routines and procedures that lead to faculty and staff perceptions of a safe, supportive, and orderly environment.

Figure 2.6: Scale for leading indicator 1.1—The faculty and staff perceive the school environment as safe, supportive, and orderly.

The performance scale in figure 2.6 is straightforward (as are all performance scales throughout the book). At the *not attempting* level, the school leader makes no attempt to address the leading indicator. At the *beginning* level, the leader has some routines and procedures in place, but he or she does not implement them schoolwide. At the *developing* level, schoolwide implementation occurs, but no monitoring. The *applying* level involves monitoring the school's performance through the use of lagging indicators and the data associated with them. At this level, the leader can legitimately say he or she has certified the school's performance for a particular indicator. The *sustaining* level involves the full HRS process because it incorporates the continuous collection of quick data and appropriate interventions when those data indicate potential problems. We refer to this as the *sustaining* level because at this point, the leader ensures the school continuously maintains the HRS principles.

In working with schools, we have noted some challenges leaders face when moving up through the levels of the performance scale for indicator 1.1. For example, many schools leave rules and procedures to the discretion of individual teachers. This works fairly well in individual classrooms but often makes students confused regarding expectations outside the classroom. In schools that have common rules and procedures in place for things like hallway behavior, lunchroom procedures, and student interactions, performance on indicator 1.1 reaches the developing level at minimum. With this leading indicator, leaders also face the challenge of lacking well-established lagging indicators. In our experience with schools, we find that schools sometimes have solid rules and procedures in place schoolwide, but schools do not have metrics in place to indicate whether those produce their desired effects. Lagging indicators help ensure that schools have appropriate metrics in place to monitor these effects.

Leading Indicator 1.2

Students, parents, and the community perceive the school environment as safe, supportive, and orderly.

Equally important to the faculty and staff's perceptions of a school's culture are the perceptions of students, parents, and the community. Many actions and procedures for this indicator might look similar to those for leading indicator 1.1, and in some cases, they may be identical. For example, the positive behavior program initiatives mentioned previously address both indicators 1.1 and 1.2. However, students, parents, and the community have some unique ways in which they can get involved in the creation of a safe and orderly environment.

One example comes from Raymond Gabaldon Elementary in Los Lunas, New Mexico. The principal, Barbara Carrillo, started a moms-and-sons group as a positive intervention strategy to help redirect some boys who get into physical or verbal altercations on a regular basis. The group meets regularly throughout the year. In these meetings, the moms and sons talk as a group about the hopes and dreams the moms have for their sons and their expectations for how their sons should conduct themselves as young men. This initiative has resulted in a decrease in discipline incidents within that particular group of boys, which, in turn, has had a calming effect across the school as a whole.

Personal projects, as described in the section on indicator 1.1 (page 44), provide ready-made opportunities for parent and community involvement. Such projects relate directly to supporting students' learning goals. When parents and the community are involved in these projects, the perception of student support broadens. Specifically, the second step of the seven-step process for personal projects involves identifying mentors and role models. We have found that students commonly identify members of their family and the local community to fill these roles. Additionally, family and community members commonly act as the audience to whom students present the fruits of their personal projects.

Lagging Indicators

As mentioned previously, lagging indicators provide concrete and sometimes quantifiable evidence that a school is meeting its leading indicators' requirements. For example, on a quarterly basis, a school could monitor results of focus groups involving students and parents conducted during that quarter.

Other lagging indicators that address leading indicator 1.2 include:

- Parents maintain an average score of 4.0 or higher on a five-point scale when they take a survey that asks them if they consider the school environment safe, supportive, and orderly.

- The school has clear protocols and procedures in place in case of emergency and has practiced them.

- The school has student mentoring programs in place to promote positive behaviors and culture.

- Climate survey data indicate that 90 percent or more of parents and students perceive the school as a safe, supportive, and orderly place.

- Parents and students receive clear procedures for drop-off before school and pickup after school.

- The school has systems by which students may anonymously report potential incidents that would indicate a lack of safety or order.

Quick Data and Continuous Improvement

To collect and analyze quick data for this indicator, a school could, for example, periodically hand out parking-lot surveys (for example, one or two questions) to parents waiting to pick up their children after school. The survey questions might include, On a five-point scale, how safe do you feel our school is, with 5 meaning *very safe*? and Do you have any specific areas of concern with school safety you would like to bring to our attention? The school then collects and aggregates the data. On average, this practice produces data from eighty to one hundred surveys.

Other examples of quick data include the following.

- The school periodically conducts student focus groups to ask students about their thoughts on school safety issues.
- The school provides parents with short surveys regarding the school's safety and orderliness while they wait in the office's reception area.
- The school nurse collects playground injury data to look for trends in student injuries.

Leader Accountability

Leader accountability for this indicator involves monitoring whether programs and practices are in place that lead to student, parent, and community perceptions of a safe, supportive, and orderly environment and that these programs and practices are having their desired effects. Figure 2.7 contains a proficiency scale leaders can use to judge their effectiveness relative to indicator 1.2.

Sustaining	Applying	Developing	Beginning	Not Attempting
The school continually cultivates information through quick data sources to monitor student, parent, and community perceptions of the safety, supportiveness, and orderliness of the school environment, and it takes proper actions to intervene when quick data indicate a potential problem.	The school has developed and implemented well-defined, schoolwide routines and procedures that lead to student, parent, and community perceptions of a safe, supportive, and orderly environment, and it can produce lagging indicators to show the desired effects of these actions.	The school has developed and implemented well-defined, schoolwide routines and procedures that lead to student, parent, and community perceptions of a safe, supportive, and orderly environment.	The school is in the beginning, yet incomplete, stages of developing and implementing well-defined, schoolwide routines and procedures that lead to student, parent, and community perceptions of a safe, supportive, and orderly environment.	The school has not attempted to develop and implement well-defined, schoolwide routines and procedures that lead to student, parent, and community perceptions of a safe, supportive, and orderly environment.

Figure 2.7: Scale for leading indicator 1.2—Students, parents, and the community perceive the school environment as safe, supportive, and orderly.

Challenges leaders face as they move through the levels of this scale include establishing schoolwide routines and procedures that students, parents, and the community can easily understand and ensuring they get enforced with a high degree of consistency. To this end, many school leaders also establish a discipline matrix to provide guidance and consistency in enforcing schoolwide procedures. Typically, leaders present this matrix to students, parents, and community members during its design and ask for input from these constituents. Additionally, as leaders create or revise schoolwide routines and procedures, they must communicate the rationale for how they will help establish a safe, supportive, and orderly school environment. Including a team of lead teachers and parents in this process makes this leading indicator much more effective and easier to implement.

Leading Indicator 1.3

Teachers have formal roles in the decision-making process regarding school initiatives.

Creating formal structures that involve teachers in specific aspects of decision making for their school represents a key aspect of leading a high reliability school. In fact, when a staff decision-making process drives specific initiatives, the initiatives can quickly gain momentum and acceptance by the whole staff. In the book *Leaders of Learning*, DuFour and Marzano (2011) state, "No single person has all the knowledge, skills, and talent to lead a district, improve a school, or meet all the needs of every child in his or her classroom" (p. 2). The Wallace Foundation report (Louis et al., 2010) also addresses the concept of shared decision making and offers the following key findings:

- Collective leadership has a stronger influence on student achievement than individual leadership.
- Almost all people associated with high-performing schools have greater influence on school decisions than is the case with people in low-performing schools.
- Higher-performing schools award greater influence to teacher teams, parents, and students, in particular.
- Principals and district leaders have the most influence on decisions in all schools; however, they do not lose influence as others gain influence.
- School leaders have an impact on student achievement primarily through their influence on teachers' motivation and working conditions; their influence on teachers' knowledge and skills produces less impact on student achievement. (p. 19)

Leaders must consider three key aspects of this leading indicator as they address it in their schools: (1) create formal structures to practice shared decision making, (2) identify the types of decisions for which they will seek teacher input, and (3) ensure transparency so the staff know and understand the shared decision-making process.

1. **Create formal structures to practice shared decision making:** At Round Rock High School in Round Rock, Texas, staff refer to the predominant structure for shared decision making as the *learning leadership team*. This team includes all administrators, all curriculum department heads, and the school's lead counselor. It leaves an open chair available to teachers from any department who are not formal team members but take an interest in the team's work or perhaps want to speak directly to an issue the team would address.

2. **Identify the types of decisions for which they will seek teacher input:** Decisions made in any school fit into three basic categories.

   a. Decisions individual teachers or teacher teams make with full autonomy

   b. Decisions in which teachers routinely have direct input

   c. Decisions school administrators make without teacher input

   School leaders can use the decision organizer in figure 2.8 to help guide their thinking on the three types of decisions. Leaders can consider specific decisions that fall into each column and list them to begin identifying which decisions will involve teachers. Over time, the decision-making process should expand to include others to ensure adequate representation from constituents. Finally, leaders should create a concise document that clearly communicates specific decision-making responsibilities.

   This one act of leadership can begin to eliminate some issues that arise when ambiguity exists regarding who has involvement in specific decisions. When such ambiguity exists, staff members often wonder why they do not get asked about or included in specific decisions. In reality, school leaders should actually involve them in making these decisions. Likewise, some issues are better addressed with staff input; those resolutions will more likely get accepted and move forward with less resistance. Leading indicator 1.3 refers to the types of decisions that fall into the middle column of figure 2.8, where administrators and teachers share responsibility.

Decisions Individual Teachers or Teacher Teams Make With Full Autonomy	Decisions in Which Teachers Routinely Have Direct Input	Decisions School Administrators Make Without Teacher Input

Figure 2.8: Decision organizer.

*Visit **go.SolutionTree.com/leadership** for a free reproducible version of this figure.*

3. **Ensure transparency so the staff know and understand the shared decision-making process:** In many schools where principals have established formal, shared decision-making structures, the only staff members who know about them are those participating in them. To avoid this trap, school leaders must develop a plan for how they will share information with the whole staff. This doesn't mean that the principal has to always share decisions with the staff him- or herself. In fact, it makes sense that some teachers involved in the decisions would be the prime candidates to formally share that information with the staff digitally or in person. For example, if all teacher-team leaders participate in a schoolwide leadership team, those team leaders should update their local teams on the shared decisions the larger team makes, and they should seek their local teams' additional input.

Lagging Indicators

A school can identify and monitor a lagging indicator for leading indicator 1.3 using a staff survey. This survey gathers data on what percentage of staff believe they have a formal role in the decision-making process regarding school initiatives. If 70 percent of staff initially perceive that they have formal roles in this process, school leaders might choose to set a lagging indicator goal of 85 percent. Leaders could then increase the roles staff have in decision making. Then, they could survey faculty and staff periodically to see if they have met the lagging indicator criterion. If the faculty and staff do not meet the criterion after that, the leaders can try other strategies.

Other lagging indicators that address leading indicator 1.3 include:

- Ninety percent of staff agree or strongly agree that they have formal roles in the decision-making process regarding school initiatives.
- Leaders make clear the types of decisions that teachers will have direct input on.
- Notes and reports describe how leaders use teacher input when making specific decisions.
- Leaders target and utilize groups of teachers to provide input regarding specific decisions.

Quick Data and Continuous Improvement

To collect and analyze quick data for this indicator, a school could, for example, have each member of its broad-based leadership team—which it refers to as its *guiding coalition*—talk with two staff members each and ask them the following two questions.

1. "Can you name a current school initiative?"
2. "How are teachers involved in decisions regarding this initiative?"

Team members then bring the responses back to the leadership team, compile the results, and look for patterns in the responses to monitor how the school does with this leading indicator.

Other examples of quick data include the following.

- Teachers identify decision-making opportunities in which they have had direct involvement.
- Teachers identify specific school initiatives that have involved them in the decision-making process.
- Leaders have quick conversations with teachers to assess their knowledge of school decisions.

Leader Accountability

Leader accountability for this indicator involves monitoring whether programs and practices are in place that lead to teachers being involved in decisions for school initiatives and that these programs and practices are having their desired effects. Leaders can examine their progress relative to this leading indicator using the proficiency scale in figure 2.9.

Sustaining	Applying	Developing	Beginning	Not Attempting
The school continually cultivates information through quick data sources to monitor teachers' formal roles and involvement in decision-making processes, and it takes proper actions to intervene when quick data indicate a potential problem.	For specific types of decisions, the school has implemented formal processes to involve teachers in the decision-making process for school initiatives, and it can produce lagging indicators to show the desired effects of these actions.	For specific types of decisions, the school has implemented formal processes to involve teachers in the decision-making process for school initiatives.	The school is in the beginning, yet incomplete, stages of implementing formal processes to involve teachers in the decision-making process for school initiatives.	The school has not attempted to implement formal processes to involve teachers in the decision-making process for school initiatives.

Figure 2.9: Scale for leading indicator 1.3—Teachers have formal roles in the decision-making process regarding school initiatives.

One of the biggest challenges leaders face as they move through the levels of this scale occurs when they have processes in place for teacher involvement in decisions, but leaders don't record or communicate the impact of these decisions with the faculty. Teachers not only want to get involved in decisions but also want to see the results of their work. If decisions provide positive outcomes, teachers want to celebrate them; if decisions provide negative outcomes, teachers want to learn from them.

Leading Indicator 1.4

Collaborative teams regularly interact to address common issues regarding curriculum, assessment, instruction, and the achievement of all students.

As mentioned in the beginning of this chapter, collaboration through the PLC process is central not only to this level of the HRS model but to all the model's levels. However, this specific indicator addresses the formal establishment of a viable way to make this happen.

In their book *Transformative Collaboration*, Tonia Flanagan, Gavin Grift, Kylie Lipscombe, Colin Sloper, and Janelle Wills (2016) identify five commitments leaders must make to lead PLC implementation.

1. Understand what it means to be a PLC.
2. Find the courage you need to lead.
3. Build a climate of trust.
4. Shape school structures for success.
5. Create clarity in collaboration.

Marvin Fairman and Leon McLean (2003) explain that effective school leaders:

> Find themselves in the dynamic position of trying to increase the capacity of individuals and teams by empowering them but at the same time recognizing their organizational responsibility to counterbalance individual and team empowerment with the requirements for hierarchical accountability. Therefore the challenge for leaders is to balance that delicate tension between empowerment from below and organizational accountability from above. (p. 46)

They refer to this dynamic as *reciprocal accountability*.

DuFour and Marzano (2011) identify a number of areas within which school leaders must practice reciprocal accountability so that their school's collaborative team network has the needed conditions for success. We address five of those areas: (1) organize staff into meaningful teams; (2) provide teams with time to collaborate; (3) provide supportive structures that help groups become teams; (4) clarify the work teams must accomplish; and (5) monitor teamwork and provide direction and support as needed.

1. **Organize staff into meaningful teams:** Marzano, Heflebower, Hoegh, Warrick, and Grift (2016) make the point that "no two schools are exactly alike in terms of what constitutes a meaningful team. The most commonly used structures are grade-level teams and content-area teams, but schools can use other organizational schemes to suit their needs" (p. 20). For example, a ninth-grade team may consist of multiple content-area teachers who share a common, overarching academic goal and a group of students, while the same school also has collaborative teams consisting of common content teams. The key lies in organizing collaborative teams in a manner that gives them a meaningful purpose for their collaboration focused on improving student learning.

2. **Provide teams with time to collaborate:** DuFour and Marzano (2011) explain, "It is perplexing to see the number of districts that proclaim the importance of staff members working collaboratively that provide neither the time nor the structure vital to collaboration" (p. 73). Providing time for collaboration is essential for becoming a high reliability school. School leaders can provide time for teacher collaboration in various ways, including by using late-start or early-out schedules and developing a master schedule that includes common planning time for teacher teams. "This can be challenging, but if a school values collaboration, allotted time is essential for putting that value into practice" (Marzano et al., 2016, p. 19).

3. **Provide supportive structures that help groups become teams:** Simply organizing people into a group that we call a *team* does not ensure they will function as a team. Flanagan et al. (2016) state:

   > Given that so much of a PLC's success is dependent on the willingness of school staff to de-privatize their practice with one another, it follows that without high levels of relational trust it will be effectively impossible to build a network of high-functioning collaborative teams. (p. 35)

   While team development occurs through the actual work teams do, school leaders can ensure they put specific structures in place to cultivate relational trust within the collaborative process. To this end, they must establish school-wide norms. As Marzano et al. (2016) note, "In our view, the entire school should operate as a PLC made up of a network of collaborative teams. Those collaborative teams, if they are to function effectively, must be linked by schoolwide norms" (p. 17).

   Schoolwide norms provide guidance for and should influence the development of individual team norms. Thus, although individual team norms might be somewhat idiosyncratic to a specific group, the schoolwide norms still anchor them. When establishing schoolwide norms, leaders need to remember *less is more*. Schoolwide norms set the overall expectations for collaboration, but they should not be so numerous that they eliminate teams' opportunity to develop their own. For example, schoolwide norms might include statements such as:

- Practice a collaborative focus on learning for all students.
- Teach and assess the guaranteed and viable curriculum.
- Drive actions with data-informed decisions.
- Practice collective wisdom and borrow each other's ideas.

4. **Clarify the work teams must accomplish:** Identifying the right work for collaborative teams and providing clear guidance as to what that work includes allow collaborative team members to be prepared and productive during the time provided. This also provides clear artifacts for school leaders to monitor as quick data sources so they know whether teams function appropriately.

As principal at Hernandez Middle School in Round Rock, Texas, Mario Acosta addressed this aspect of reciprocal accountability through a PLC collaborative cycle that clearly identifies the work teams must accomplish in the context of unit planning through the four critical questions of a PLC (DuFour, DuFour, Eaker, Many, & Mattos, 2016). Figure 2.10 shows the planning cycle. Not only does this cycle clarify the work of collaborative teams, it also allows school leaders to review authentic artifacts of a team's collaboration.

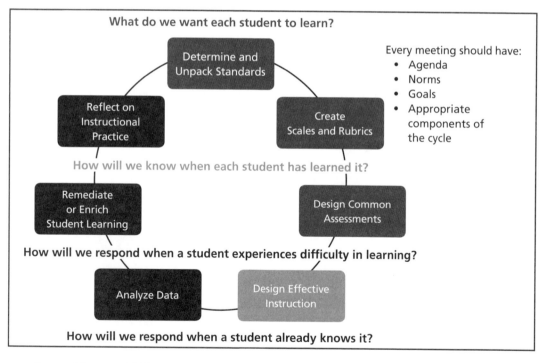

Source: Marzano, 2015.

Figure 2.10: PLC unit planning cycle.

5. **Monitor teamwork and provide direction and support as needed:**
Through their collaborative work, teams develop artifacts of practice that flow from the dialogue of a team engaged in collective inquiry on the right work.

School leaders should periodically collect and review these artifacts as sources of quick data. As a result, they can monitor the work teams do and look for areas in which individual teams might need support. These artifacts should not create additional work for the teams but rather provide authentic samples of the specific work the teams do. These might include copies of common assessments, proficiency scales, common assessment results, intervention plans, or team-created instructional plans.

If school leaders have clearly communicated the work teams should do, these artifacts will tell the story of how a team is progressing or not progressing in the work. Many school leaders fall into the trap of assuming that because the school has the team structures in place, the work is happening. The old cliché "What is measured will get done" applies in this case. School leaders should periodically audit collaborative teams by collecting and reviewing specific artifacts of practice.

Lagging Indicators

A school can identify and monitor a lagging indicator for leading indicator 1.4 by having team digital folders that contain artifacts of each collaborative team's work throughout the year. The school administration periodically audits the folders and celebrates artifacts of outstanding practice with those teams to reinforce the right work.

Other lagging indicators that address leading indicator 1.4 include:

- Collaborative teams meet weekly (at a minimum) and spend 90 percent of their meeting time discussing and working on curriculum, instruction, and assessment.
- The school designs its schedule to allow for collaborative time within the contractual workday.
- The school makes available or displays copies of schoolwide norms and individual team norms.
- The school makes available copies of common assessments created by collaborative teams.
- The school outlines a specific collaborative process to guide teams in their work.
- The school uses data walls to monitor student achievement by grade level, subject area, and even team.

Quick Data and Continuous Improvement

To collect and analyze quick data for this indicator, administrators could, for example, have each team take a turn reporting on its current work to the rest of the staff during monthly staff meetings. Each collaborative team provides a thirty-second update that includes the specific content it has focused on, the results of any formative assessments it has given, or any intervention strategies it has used. As teams provide their updates, the administrators listen and ask clarifying questions when needed.

Other examples of quick data include the following.

- When asked, teachers describe the specific collaborative work occurring in their teams at any given time.
- Common assessment results are available upon request.
- Teachers describe specific academic intervention strategies their teams implement based on student data.
- The school uses data walls to continually monitor student progress by grade level, team, and even teacher.

Leader Accountability

Leader accountability for this indicator involves monitoring whether programs and practices are in place that lead to collaborative teams meeting regularly to address issues regarding curriculum, instruction, assessment, and student achievement and that these programs and practices are having their desired effects. Leaders can evaluate their effectiveness using the proficiency scale in figure 2.11.

Sustaining	Applying	Developing	Beginning	Not Attempting
The school continually cultivates information through quick data sources to monitor the work of teacher teams and collaborative groups relative to their work on curriculum, instruction, assessment, and student achievement, and it takes proper actions to intervene when quick data indicate a potential problem.	The school has established formal, schoolwide processes for teacher teams and collaborative groups to meet regularly to address issues regarding curriculum, instruction, assessment, and student achievement, and it can produce lagging indicators to show the desired effects of these actions.	The school has established formal, schoolwide processes for teacher teams and collaborative groups to meet regularly to address issues regarding curriculum, instruction, assessment, and student achievement.	The school is in the beginning, yet incomplete, stages of establishing formal, schoolwide processes for teacher teams and collaborative groups to meet regularly to address issues regarding curriculum, instruction, assessment, and student achievement.	The school has not attempted to establish formal, schoolwide processes for teacher teams and collaborative groups to meet regularly to address issues regarding curriculum, instruction, assessment, and student achievement.

Figure 2.11: Scale for leading indicator 1.4—Collaborative teams regularly interact to address common issues regarding curriculum, assessment, instruction, and the achievement of all students.

Challenges leaders face as they move through the levels of this scale include organizing staff into collaborative teams. This may present difficulties when school leaders try to decide what to do with singleton teachers or teachers who teach different courses within like content areas, such as fine arts. To get past this hurdle, remember that not all teams need to look alike or do the exact same work. When organizing teams, leaders should keep in mind that the teams must each have a clear focus on improving student learning and growing their own effectiveness as teachers. But that does not mean each team must engage in the same type of work.

Another type of challenge occurs in providing time for teams to collaborate. If at all possible, this time should fit within the contractual day, even if it means revising the schedule on a frequent basis to take advantage of serendipitous opportunities for teams to meet.

Once a school has collaborative structures in place, school leaders must continually monitor the quick data to look for errors, and not take for granted that professional collaboration will continue consistently across all teams in a school.

Leading Indicator 1.5

Teachers and staff have formal ways to provide input regarding the optimal functioning of the school.

Although it looks similar on the surface, this leading indicator differs from leading indicator 1.3, as it refers not to formal decision making but rather to formal ways for teachers and staff to put forth ideas for consideration. As Fairman and McLean (2003) state, "The effectiveness of organizations is impacted by the degree to which they have an effective and consistent method of responding to internal and external problems, issues, and concerns" (p. 33). Formal structures and protocols for input are the critical aspects in this indicator that allow school leaders to respond to problems, issues, and concerns.

With the creation of formal structures, school leaders clearly communicate the pathway staff members can and should use to put forth their thoughts for consideration on any and all issues regarding the school's operations. Often, school leaders assume staff and teachers will share ideas with them informally, which in many cases might be true, but not in all cases and certainly not for all staff members. Establishing formal structures and clearly communicating them to teachers and staff demonstrate that school leaders are open to ideas and input.

Using something as simple as a suggestion box and corresponding suggestion forms can serve as a powerful strategy for this purpose. For example, one high school principal created a form titled "Little Things, Big Differences." On this form, any teacher or staff member can make suggestions for improving the school's operations as long as he or she doesn't just issue a complaint.

Technology provides some easy and effective ways to implement this leading indicator. If school leaders plan to use suggestion-box technology, they should consider whether the technology provides for anonymity, as some people find anonymity important when giving suggestions. For example, an online tool called Suggestion Ox (www.suggestionox.com) features anonymous suggestion technology.

Within this leading indicator, school leaders must transparently acknowledge ideas put forth through the formal process. They can do this by providing whole-staff feedback or individual feedback to the people who submitted a suggestion, if they did not submit it anonymously.

This does not mean leaders should accept and implement every suggestion or idea provided. To the contrary, this indicator allows school leaders to decline suggestions. But school leaders must explain to teachers and staff that they considered their ideas and provide their rationale for why they implemented, modified, or declined the ideas. This practice completes the cycle of communication. Too often, full communication does not occur, which creates the perception that the school leaders do not value teacher and staff input.

Lagging Indicators

A school can identify and monitor a lagging indicator for leading indicator 1.5 by listing all the ways staff can provide input and sharing specific examples of staff input. Staff find such a document useful because it allows them to see all the formal ways they can provide input. Once the list is complete, if staff do not feel they have enough ways to provide input, leaders can explore additional input avenues.

Other lagging indicators that address leading indicator 1.5 include:

- Eighty-five percent of the staff agree that teachers have formal ways to provide input regarding the optimal functioning of the school.
- The school archives data regarding ideas that teachers and staff put forth through established formal structures.
- School leaders keep notes to document when the school receives formal input and how it acts on that input.
- The school provides formal feedback to staff regarding input provided and how it considered the feedback for implementation.

Quick Data and Continuous Improvement

To collect and analyze quick data for this indicator, a school could, for example, have three members of the school leadership team keep a list of all the ways they see or hear staff provide input over a four-week period. At the end of the month, these three staff members share their findings with the school leadership team and discuss whether they believe an appropriate amount of input is occurring based on their quick data.

Other examples of quick data include the following.

- Teachers recall specific feedback provided to the staff regarding input received and considered.
- Teachers identify specific times they have provided formal input regarding the optimal functioning of the school.
- Leaders offer quick conversations with teachers to assess their knowledge of the formal input structures available in the school.

Leader Accountability

Leader accountability for this indicator involves monitoring whether programs and practices are in place that lead to formal processes for teachers and staff to provide input regarding optimal school functioning and that these programs and practices are having their desired effects. Leaders can evaluate their effectiveness using the proficiency scale in figure 2.12.

Sustaining	Applying	Developing	Beginning	Not Attempting
The school continually cultivates information through quick data sources to monitor formal structures for teachers and staff to provide input regarding optimal school functioning, and it takes proper actions to intervene when quick data indicate a potential problem.	The school has implemented formal processes for teachers and staff to provide input regarding optimal school functioning, and it can produce lagging indicators to show the desired effects of these actions.	The school has implemented formal processes for teachers and staff to provide input regarding optimal school functioning.	The school is in the beginning, yet incomplete, stages of implementing formal processes for teachers and staff to provide input regarding optimal school functioning.	The school has not attempted to implement formal processes for teachers and staff to provide input regarding optimal school functioning.

Figure 2.12: Scale for leading indicator 1.5—Teachers and staff have formal ways to provide input regarding the optimal functioning of the school.

Challenges leaders face as they move through the levels of this scale include making sure that staff have awareness of all the opportunities they have to provide input. For example, one high school established two good opportunities staff could use for this purpose. First, it distributed an input form titled "Consider This" that staff could fill out and submit to the office. Second, it held a quarterly, face-to-face, open input session that any teacher could attend to discuss school issues and ideas for improvement. Although both of these opportunities were good strategies, administrators only mentioned them early in the year during back-to-school meetings and never reminded staff of their existence during the year. Many new teachers had to deal with so much information they missed these opportunities altogether, and others forgot that these opportunities existed.

Also, leaders face the challenge of communicating back to staff that they received the staff's input. For example, in one high school, leaders routinely sought staff input on a variety of issues. However, when surveyed, the staff indicated otherwise. The problem came from the lack of feedback that leaders provided to staff to help them recognize how the school used their input. The principal basically acknowledged this lack of feedback, saying he assumed people would recognize their input when it went into practice.

Finally, we have seen leaders make the mistake of not communicating to staff why they do not implement certain staff suggestions. In one instance, a group of teachers made a suggestion to change the high school's testing schedule for end-of-semester exams. The suggestion came forward in a face-to-face conversation between one teacher and the assistant principal. After reviewing the suggestion, the administration determined that it would not implement it because of the student transportation schedule, which involved a number of bus routes that also served other schools. In this instance, the administrators simply continued with the current schedule and did not communicate why they did not make the change. As a result, they gave several teachers the false impression that the school had not considered the teachers' input, when, in fact, it had deeply considered the input.

Leading Indicator 1.6

Students, parents, and the community have formal ways to provide input regarding the optimal functioning of the school.

For this leading indicator, school leaders must create specific and formal ways for students, parents, and the community to provide their input to the school. Although some parents will email, call, or come to school to express their opinions to school leaders, this leading indicator puts the school back in control of how this input process occurs. Also, this indicator communicates that these groups' opinions matter to school leaders and that school leaders formally seek these opinions. As we stated with leading indicator 1.5, although these groups have important opinions, school leaders should weigh their input's content, topic, and legitimacy to decide whether to implement the suggestions.

Leaders can use technology in many ways for this purpose. Quick response (QR) codes that link directly to specific survey questions represent an easy-to-use option. For example, in order to actively seek parent input, Virginia Reinhardt Elementary School in Rockwall, Texas, uses a QR code that links directly to a short parent survey. While parents wait in the office, perhaps to pick up their children for an appointment, they can use the QR code and provide input to the school. In addition, as noted in leading indicator 1.5, web-based suggestion-box applications such as Suggestion Ox (www.suggestionox.com) are easy to set up and provide an efficient way to collect opinions or ideas. Of course, using a traditional suggestion box for this purpose can prove equally effective as long as someone monitors it regularly.

Lagging Indicators

A school can identify and monitor a lagging indicator for leading indicator 1.6 by reviewing parent or community input received each month. Additionally, school leadership can establish minimum acceptable levels of input per month. For example, the school might set the criterion of at least twenty-five communications per month from parents and community.

Other lagging indicators that address leading indicator 1.6 include:

- Eighty percent of parents can name at least one way they can provide input regarding the optimal functioning of the school.
- The school has data-collection systems in place to collect opinion data from students, parents, and the community regarding the optimal functioning of the school.
- The school leader conducts focus group meetings with students and parents.
- The school leader uses a web-based application to collect opinions from the community regarding specific issues.

Quick Data and Continuous Improvement

To collect and analyze quick data for this indicator, a school could, for example, pay attention to the feedback it receives in parent focus groups. In one school, the principal and assistant principal alternated conducting parent-input focus groups every other month. Leaders randomly selected parents for the focus groups and then formally invited them to attend with a mailed invitation, which also contained an agenda of the discussion topics. They sent fifteen invitations for each focus group. In one situation, during the first semester, the focus-group participation rate was slightly higher than 80 percent. During the second semester, the participation rate dropped to just more than 60 percent, which helped the school realize the first three to four months of school signified the prime time for parent input.

Other examples of quick data include the following.

- Parents can identify formal ways they can provide their opinions.
- Students can identify when they have been included in focus groups to share their opinions.
- Students can identify specific issues about which school leaders or teachers have sought their opinions.

Leader Accountability

Leader accountability for this indicator involves monitoring whether programs and practices are in place that lead to formal processes for students, parents, and the community to provide input regarding the optimal functioning of the school and that these programs and practices are having their desired effects. Leaders can evaluate their effectiveness using the proficiency scale in figure 2.13.

Sustaining	Applying	Developing	Beginning	Not Attempting
The school continually cultivates information through quick data sources to monitor formal structures for students, parents, and the community to provide input regarding optimal school functioning, and it takes proper actions to intervene when quick data indicate a potential problem.	The school has implemented formal processes for students, parents, and the community to provide input regarding optimal school functioning, and it can produce lagging indicators to show the desired effects of these actions.	The school has implemented formal processes for students, parents, and the community to provide input regarding optimal school functioning.	The school is in the beginning, yet incomplete, stages of implementing formal processes for students, parents, and the community to provide input regarding optimal school functioning.	The school has not attempted to implement formal processes for students, parents, and the community to provide input regarding optimal school functioning.

Figure 2.13: Scale for leading indicator 1.6—Students, parents, and the community have formal ways to provide input regarding the optimal functioning of the school.

As leaders move through this scale, they may face challenges when initially establishing formal methods of input and getting students, parents, and the community in the habit of using these methods. To illustrate, one elementary school set up a parent suggestion box in the office and made parents aware of its existence. However, for the first two months, it received only three submissions. The school then decided to move to a digital suggestion-box format, which the parents and community found easier to use.

Getting input from specific demographic groups also poses a challenge due to language or cultural barriers. For example, a high school that served a large group of families from the former Soviet Union found that parents were not accustomed to having any input at school because it did not meet their cultural norms.

A final challenge involves communicating with students, parents, and the community to let them know the school received their input. To remedy this, one high school principal created a section in his monthly newsletter dedicated specifically to providing feedback on different suggestions he had received from parents and the community. He listed the suggestions he had received that month, followed by a short narrative about what the school did in response to them.

Leading Indicator 1.7

The school acknowledges the success of the whole school as well as individuals within the school.

Appropriately recognizing the contributions and successes of people within an organization is critical for maintaining a healthy culture. In their book *How Full Is Your Bucket?*, Tom Rath and Donald Clifton (2005) cite Gallup research that indicates when employees receive regular recognition and praise, they demonstrate increased individual productivity and engagement with their colleagues, and they are more likely to stay with the organization.

We must consider several critical leadership behaviors to effectively address this indicator. First, school leaders must ensure they appropriately recognize individuals and have various strategies for doing it. To this end, school leaders should take the time to find out which staff members feel comfortable being celebrated publicly and which feel more comfortable being celebrated privately. Certainly, some faculty members and some students do not feel comfortable as the focus of a public celebration. However, something as simple but genuine as a personal note or letter celebrating success can have a strong impact.

Second, school leaders should celebrate specific actions and accomplishments that exemplify quality practice, and not only celebrate an individual because his or her turn has come. The things leaders celebrate send a clear message about their expectations. Therefore, leaders should celebrate practices and accomplishments they want to see replicated in their schools.

Third, leaders must make sure they provide ample opportunities to recognize and celebrate all students and staff members. Establishing protocols for recognizing students for success in multiple aspects of student life ensures that leaders do not overcelebrate certain students or certain aspects of student life while ignoring others. The same holds true for recognizing teachers' and staff members' success in all the areas that have critical significance to the school's functioning.

This indicator also provides schools with an opportunity to create recognitions that are unique and important to their overall mission and culture. The following examples demonstrate practices from two different schools that have personalized their implementation of this leading indicator.

Midwest City High School in Midwest City, Oklahoma (home of the Bombers), employs a student recognition system in which teachers and administrators identify students each month for its Bomber Magic program. The acronym *MAGIC* represents important characteristics the school wants to develop in students, which include manners, ambition, grit, integrity, and confidence. Nominated students receive an award certificate based on the specific characteristic they exhibit (L. Broiles, personal communication, September 8, 2015). Figure 2.14 shows an example of one of those certificates. The second example in figure 2.14 shows how Deer Creek Elementary School in the Deer Creek School District in Oklahoma offers opportunities for staff members to recognize their peers by filling each other's bucket with notes of appreciation (L. Padgett, personal communication, February 6, 2017).

Source: © 2015 by Midwest City High School. Used with permission.

Figure 2.14: Examples of recognition.

Lagging Indicators

A school can identify and monitor a lagging indicator for leading indicator 1.7 by creating a list of things it celebrates, a list of things it should celebrate, and guidelines for the amount of time and expense associated with celebrations. Leaders then monitor and set expectations for the number of celebrations per quarter. Obviously, some celebrations happen more spontaneously based on real-time events, but leaders can plan others ahead of time. For example, during times when school achievement data become available, leaders can plan and schedule celebrations. Although school achievement data on the whole might not always call for celebration, leaders can almost always find notable accomplishments in subgroups, specific subject areas, or even topics within subject areas to celebrate.

Other lagging indicators that address leading indicator 1.7 include:

- Ninety percent of students and staff agree that they receive recognition for a job well done.
- The school has specific descriptions and protocols in place for recognizing and celebrating students.
- The school has specific descriptions and protocols in place for recognizing and celebrating staff.
- Artifacts of recognition and celebration are visible in the school.

Quick Data and Continuous Improvement

To collect and analyze quick data for this indicator, a school could, for example, have one grade level or department monitor the number of times it sees or has awareness of individuals, teams, or the school as a whole receiving recognition for a job well done over a two-week period. It then shares these data with the school leadership team.

Other examples of quick data include the following.

- Students explain different ways they and their peers are recognized and celebrated at school.
- Staff identify colleagues who have received recognition and the reasons for their recognition.
- Focus group data indicate parents are aware of specific ways their children receive recognition in school.

Leader Accountability

Leader accountability for this indicator involves monitoring whether programs and practices are in place that lead to acknowledging and celebrating the accomplishments of the whole school and individuals within the school and that these programs and practices are having their desired effects. Leaders can evaluate their effectiveness using the proficiency scale in figure 2.15.

Sustaining	Applying	Developing	Beginning	Not Attempting
The school continually cultivates information through quick data sources to monitor the extent to which people feel acknowledged and celebrated for their contributions, and it takes proper actions to intervene when quick data indicate a potential problem.	The school has protocols and practices in place to acknowledge and celebrate the accomplishments of the whole school and individuals within the school, and it can produce lagging indicators to show the desired effects of these actions.	The school has protocols and practices in place to acknowledge and celebrate the accomplishments of the whole school and individuals within the school.	The school is in the beginning, yet incomplete, stages of drafting protocols and practices to acknowledge and celebrate the accomplishments of the whole school and individuals within the school.	The school has not attempted to acknowledge and celebrate the accomplishments of the whole school and individuals within the school.

Figure 2.15: Scale for leading indicator 1.7—The school acknowledges the success of the whole school as well as individuals within the school.

As leaders move through this scale, they will face a challenge if they celebrate team and school accomplishments but not individual accomplishments. Sometimes, leaders are reluctant to recognize an individual even though he or she has taken clearly noteworthy individual actions. To illustrate, imagine a teacher who ensured that all students in her class reached their academic growth goals for the year. Although all team members certainly play a part in all students' success, it is still appropriate to celebrate the individual teacher in a situation like this. Not doing so could cause the teacher to not feel valued for his or her extra efforts.

Another challenge occurs when a school recognizes and celebrates individuals but not teacher teams. Teams should work in a highly collaborative environment. When a school does not recognize and honor team accomplishments, this could send the message that the school doesn't view team accomplishments as critical to the school's mission.

Leading Indicator 1.8

The school manages its fiscal, operational, and technological resources in a way that directly supports teachers.

Leaders must manage multiple resources that directly and indirectly support teachers in the classroom. While conversations about resources often center on fiscal resources, school leaders must also focus on management of other types of resources to support teaching and learning. For example, school leaders need to manage operational resources because they hold great potential for improving teaching and learning, and every school possesses specific operational resources.

One key operational resource is a school's master schedule. School leaders should continually evaluate how they might allocate time in the school day to support teaching and learning. For example, the principal at Waverly High School in Waverly, Nebraska, employed a flexible schedule for freshman cross-curricular teams, which allowed each team to decide how to use a block of time from first through fourth period each day. Teacher teams had the flexibility to meet in equal increments of time for each core subject or to cover specific content areas longer than others based on the teaching and learning activities planned for each content area.

Using this strategy, teacher teams could allocate time to support learning in different ways, such as organizing assessment of a larger group to create extended time for other content area instruction. For example, students on this team start their day by taking the world history assessment at the same time. However, they might be taking it in their mathematics or science classroom in a smaller group setting because the team planned it that way and allocated thirty minutes in each classroom that served that group of students. Once the assessment time is finished, the world history teachers immediately begin scoring the assessment, and there is no need for students to rotate through their history class now as they have already completed the test. This provides other core content area teachers additional time with students on that day so they can plan small-group interventions or engage students in learning activities that require some additional time.

Teachers can use this same strategy to provide additional time in a specific content area. For example, science teachers could ask to have ten minutes of extended time in each of their rotations on a specific day to make sure they have enough time to conduct an experiment with each class. To allow that additional time, the other content areas cut their time for that day by ten minutes each, and science absorbs that time to conduct the experiments.

School leaders also need to manage their schools' technological resources. They must create structures and protocols to ensure staff use these resources correctly. One of the most important technological resources school leaders must plan for is the availability of people who support technology in their schools. Too often, schools acquire technology or access to technology but do not account for how they will support the use and upkeep of these resources. To confound this problem, many schools do not have access to enough staff members who have the time or knowledge to do this work. To address this issue, leaders must consider different options, including using student assistants within specific parameters.

Lagging Indicators

A school can identify and monitor a lagging indicator for leading indicator 1.8 by developing *we need* lists that teachers can fill out at the end of the school year in anticipation of the next year. Teachers can request specific supplies and resources they need in their classrooms for the following year and rank those needs in order of priority. Administrators then purchase as many requested items as they can within their budget based on teachers' top priorities. When teachers return at the start of the school year, they use the list to ensure they received the items purchased and then sign off on the list and return it to the principal.

Other lagging indicators that address leading indicator 1.8 include:

- Eighty percent of teachers indicate they have resources they need to effectively teach.

- The school leader accesses and leverages a variety of resources (for example, grants and title funds).

- The school has budgets and protocols in place for teachers to access technology for teaching and learning.

- The school designs the schedule to maximize opportunities for teaching and learning.

Quick Data and Continuous Improvement

To collect and analyze quick data for this indicator, a school could, for example, monitor technology use in the classroom through a quick review of laptop carts' checkout forms. These forms indicate how often teachers check out the laptops for classroom use and the specific content areas and courses in which they use the laptops.

Other examples of quick data include the following.

- Teachers identify specific resources provided to support their teaching practices.

- Budget information indicates specific resources purchased to support classroom practices.

- Teachers describe specific technology training they receive to support technology use in the classroom.

Leader Accountability

Leader accountability for this indicator involves monitoring whether programs and practices are in place that lead to managing fiscal, operational, and technological resources in a way that supports teachers and that these programs and practices are having their desired effects. Leaders can evaluate their effectiveness using the proficiency scale in figure 2.16.

Sustaining	Applying	Developing	Beginning	Not Attempting
The school continually cultivates information through quick data sources to monitor the extent to which fiscal, operational, and technological resources support teachers, and it takes proper actions to intervene when quick data indicate a potential problem.	The school manages fiscal, operational, and technological resources in a way that supports teachers, and it can produce lagging indicators to show the desired effects of these actions.	The school manages fiscal, operational, and technological resources in a way that supports teachers.	The school is in the beginning, yet incomplete, stages of managing fiscal, operational, and technological resources in a way that supports teachers.	The school has not attempted to manage fiscal, operational, and technological resources in a way that supports teachers.

Figure 2.16: Scale for leading indicator 1.8—The school manages its fiscal, operational, and technological resources in a way that directly supports teachers.

Challenges leaders face as they move through the levels of this scale include getting stuck on the fiscal aspect of this leading indicator. Although that is a natural thing to do, especially considering the tightness of budgets, school leaders should focus more on their operational and technological resources because they have much more control of those resources, and creatively allocating these resources can provide classroom support. In other words, finances and technology are not the only ways to support teachers. Providing teachers with control over resources can result in highly creative forms of support generated by the teachers themselves.

While technology is certainly an important resource for all schools, some schools do not have nearly as many technological resources as others have. School leaders can mitigate this challenge by creatively allocating existing technology and using *bring your own device* initiatives that allow specific programs to strategically allocate technological resources.

Level 1 Transformations

Level 1 of the HRS model deals with factors that are foundational to a well-functioning school. Who would question the importance of safety, support, and collaboration? As mundane as these factors seem, we have found that directly attending to them in the form of leading and lagging indicators embedded in the HRS process can produce profound and sometimes unanticipated results. Following are a few examples.

Kristy VanDorn, principal at Deer Creek Middle School in Edmond, Oklahoma, became a new principal at the same time that the Deer Creek School District was implementing the HRS model. As she explains, she learned a lot about leadership and school culture from the HRS model:

As a new principal, HRS has been a powerful instruction manual for me. Often new principals have no idea where to start in their new leadership role. There is a lot of uncertainty about which issues to tackle first. The HRS program provided me with direction and steps to take at each level that are research-proven and time-tested. I like how HRS provides the guidance for each level, but it doesn't tell you exactly how to implement each strategy. You can mold their strategies into what will work for your school culture. (K. VanDorn, personal communication, March 16, 2017)

In 2013, the Los Lunas, New Mexico, school district created a district-level advocate team to work with and directly support each school in the district. As the district began to implement the HRS framework, superintendent Dana Sanders asked the district advocate team to use the HRS framework as a common focus for the schools they support across the district. The power of this approach allows common expectations for each school while still allowing differentiation for the needs of individual schools as they work toward certification in the first three levels of HRS. In 2016, the district saw improvement in nearly all schools, as eight of the district's schools increased their state school grade by two or more state accountability levels and two schools increased by one accountability level in the New Mexico school grades report (D. Sanders, personal communication, September 12, 2016).

Dirk DeBoer was introduced to the HRS model as an assistant principal at Herbert Henry Dow High School in Midland, Michigan. The following year, he implemented the HRS process at Midland's Northeast Middle School after being selected as the school's principal. Here, DeBoer speaks directly about HRS level 1 work and its effect on his new school:

> In year 1 at Northeast Middle School, staff completed a level 1 survey prior to the beginning of the school year. The staff identified a need to tighten up procedures, involve more staff input in decisions, and have a system for meaningful collaboration. As a result, we improved consistency with student discipline, implemented [the PLC process], and formed two advisory teams with specific purposes (teacher support and coaching and PLC leadership). Not only have these changes improved the morale and instruction at Northeast tremendously, but we also have a solid foundation to work toward higher outcomes. (D. DeBoer, personal communication, August 20, 2017)

Conclusion

Leadership for level 1 of the HRS model focuses on creating a safe, supportive, and collaborative culture. Such an emphasis addresses the second big idea of the PLC process—a collaborative culture. This level has eight leading indicators. For a school to declare itself highly reliable relative to level 1, leaders must generate lagging indicators with clear criteria for success. Even after the school has met these success criteria, it must still continue to collect quick data to monitor and react to variations in its performance on the eight indicators.

Chapter 3

Effective Teaching in Every Classroom

• • •

Level 2 of the HRS model focuses on effective teaching in every classroom. This, of course, aligns directly with question 5 of the six critical questions Rick described in the introductory chapter: How will we increase our instructional competence?

A number of high visibility studies have demonstrated the impact a teacher has on students' learning and, by inference, the importance of helping teachers continuously improve their instructional prowess. For example, in the late 1990s, S. Paul Wright, Sandra Horn, and William Sanders (1997) conducted a study that involved the achievement of some sixty thousand students across grades 3 and 5. In the study, Wright et al. (1997) conclude:

> The most important factor affecting student learning is the teacher. In addition, the results show wide variation in effectiveness among teachers. The immediate and clear implication of this finding is that seemingly more can be done to improve education by improving the effectiveness of teachers than by any other single factor. (p. 63)

Kati Haycock (1998) explains that this study's findings prove most revealing when used to contrast the differences in learning between two students of equal ability taught by two different teachers: one teacher highly effective, and the other highly ineffective. Haycock (1998) determines that the student taught by the highly effective teacher would experience an 83 percentile point gain in learning, and the student taught by the highly ineffective teacher would experience a 29 percentile point gain in learning. About this, Haycock (1998) notes that "Differences of this magnitude—50 percentile points—are stunning. As all of us know only too well, they can represent the difference between a 'remedial' label and placement in the 'accelerated' or even 'gifted' track" (p. 4).

Because of the breadth and level of rigor of their work, Barbara Nye, Spyros Konstantopoulos, and Larry Hedges (2004) have written perhaps the most commonly cited study revealing teachers' impact on student learning. They summarize their findings as follows:

> These findings would suggest that the difference in achievement gains between having a 25th percentile teacher (a not so effective teacher) and a 75th percentile teacher (an effective teacher) is over one-third of a standard deviation (0.35) in reading and almost half a standard deviation (0.48) in mathematics. . . . These effects are certainly large enough to have policy significance. (Nye et al., 2004, p. 253)

While this research makes it clear that highly competent teachers are key to a school's ability to enhance student learning, the research does not make it clear how a school helps teachers continually develop to higher and higher levels of competence. Stated in HRS terminology, the research does not provide guidance as to the leading indicators for fostering effective teaching in every classroom. That is, the research does not make it clear how a school organizes itself to ensure all teachers reach and exceed competence in the teaching process.

The leading indicators for level 2 of the HRS model provide direction and guidance relative to this issue. When school leaders successfully address this level's indicators, it becomes nearly impossible for teachers not to grow more effective in their instructional practices. Even those teachers who would rather not engage in pedagogical growth will find it difficult to sit on the sidelines in a school that successfully implements the leading indicators for this level of the HRS model.

Level 2 of the HRS model has six leading indicators.

2.1 The school communicates a clear vision as to how teachers should address instruction.

2.2 The school supports teachers to continually enhance their pedagogical skills through reflection and professional growth plans.

2.3 The school is aware of and monitors predominant instructional practices.

2.4 The school provides teachers with clear, ongoing evaluations of their pedagogical strengths and weaknesses that are based on multiple sources of data and are consistent with student achievement data.

2.5 The school provides teachers with job-embedded professional development that is directly related to their instructional growth goals.

2.6 Teachers have opportunities to observe and discuss effective teaching.

Leading Indicator 2.1

The school communicates a clear vision as to how teachers should address instruction.

This leading indicator is the gatekeeper for success at level 2. Instructional leadership research explicitly supports the importance of having a clear vision and a common language and model of instructional practice in a school. The Wallace Foundation's Learning From Leadership Project identifies a focus on effective instructional strategies as important to school achievement overall: "How do high-scoring principals establish a vision for the school that is centered on high student achievement? For one thing, they emphasize the value of research-based strategies" (as cited in Louis et al., 2010, p. 84). Likewise, Robert Marzano, Tony Frontier, and David Livingston (2011) state, "A knowledge base for teaching is the first step a district or school must take if it is to support the development of teacher expertise" (p. 29). Marzano and Waters (2009) indicate that effective school leaders attend to developing a common vocabulary about effective practice.

To cultivate effective instruction in every classroom, school leaders first need to establish a common language or instructional practice model. In essence, a school needs to have a clear playbook for what will occur to help students learn in the classroom. The school should base its instructional model in the research on effective practices and clearly communicate the model.

In order to facilitate teacher growth, a school should make its model of instruction comprehensive. A comprehensive model allows teachers of all levels of expertise opportunities for improvement. Whereas experts within any complex domain like teaching have a wide variety of strategies to apply to their craft, novices have a relatively small set of applicable strategies. Therefore, the instructional model a school uses for this indicator should include a great many instructional strategies.

To illustrate, we use the instructional model from *The New Art and Science of Teaching* (Marzano, 2017), as shown in table 3.1 (page 78). This model contains forty-three elements embedded in ten categories. These ten categories are then embedded in three overarching groups: (1) feedback, (2) content, and (3) context.

Table 3.1: *The New Art and Science of Teaching* **Instructional Model**

Feedback	Content	Context
Providing and Communicating Clear Learning Goals 1. Providing scales and rubrics 2. Tracking student progress 3. Celebrating success **Using Assessments** 4. Using informal assessments of the whole class 5. Using formal assessments of individual students	**Conducting Direct Instruction Lessons** 6. Chunking content 7. Processing content 8. Recording and representing content **Conducting Practicing and Deepening Lessons** 9. Using structured practice sessions 10. Examining similarities and differences 11. Examining errors in reasoning **Conducting Knowledge Application Lessons** 12. Engaging students in cognitively complex tasks 13. Providing resources and guidance 14. Generating and defending claims **Using Strategies That Appear in All Types of Lessons** 15. Previewing strategies 16. Highlighting critical information 17. Reviewing content 18. Revising knowledge 19. Reflecting on learning 20. Assigning purposeful homework 21. Elaborating on information 22. Organizing students to interact	**Using Engagement Strategies** 23. Noticing and reacting when students are not engaged 24. Increasing response rates 25. Using physical movement 26. Maintaining a lively pace 27. Demonstrating intensity and enthusiasm 28. Presenting unusual information 29. Using friendly controversy 30. Using academic games 31. Providing opportunities for students to talk about themselves 32. Motivating and inspiring students **Implementing Rules and Procedures** 33. Establishing rules and procedures 34. Organizing the physical layout of the classroom 35. Demonstrating withitness 36. Acknowledging adherence to rules and procedures 37. Acknowledging lack of adherence to rules and procedures **Building Relationships** 38. Using verbal and nonverbal behaviors that indicate affection for students 39. Understanding students' backgrounds and interests 40. Displaying objectivity and control **Communicating High Expectations** 41. Demonstrating value and respect for reluctant learners 42. Asking in-depth questions of reluctant learners 43. Probing incorrect answers with reluctant learners

Source: Marzano, 2017, p. 8.

It is important to note that each of the forty-three elements includes a number of specific strategies that table 3.1 does not list. For example, element 24 (increasing response rates) includes the following nine specific strategies.

1. Random names
2. Hand signals
3. Response cards
4. Response chaining
5. Paired response
6. Choral response
7. Wait time
8. Elaborative interrogation
9. Multiple types of questions

For this indicator, the principal and other administrators in the school must function as the lead learners and develop a strong understanding of the instructional strategies they expect to see. This does not mean school leaders must grasp all pedagogical knowledge in the language of instruction, but they do need to know how to successfully speak about the expected instructional strategies with confidence and understanding.

School leaders should articulate their school's language of instruction in a hardcopy document so teachers can easily refer to it. Too often, when a document like this only exists in a digital format, it falls victim to the "out of sight, out of mind" phenomenon and is easily forgotten.

We have found that some school leaders prefer to communicate the school's model of instruction in the form of an instructional snapshot, as shown in figure 3.1 (page 80). This format is clear and concise, and teachers can use the snapshot document as a quick reference guide to remind themselves of the instructional strategies school leaders should see and hear them use almost daily, on occasion, and not at all.

Should See and Hear Almost Daily	Might See and Hear	Should Not See and Hear
<ul><li>Clear learning goals and scales</li><li>Clear classroom routines and procedures</li><li>Formative assessment of individual students and the whole class</li><li>Content chunked into digestible bites</li><li>Teacher withitness</li><li>Teachers noticing and reacting when students are disengaged</li><li>Student small-group discussion strategies</li><li>Quality and timely feedback</li><li>Questioning strategies<ul><li>Random selection to include all students</li><li>Use of wait time</li><li>Use of multiple types of questions</li><li>Prompts for elaboration on information</li></ul></li></ul>	<ul><li>Previewed content</li><li>Students tracking their own progress in learning</li><li>Academic games</li><li>Academic vocabulary instruction</li><li>Examination of similarities and differences</li><li>Examination of errors in reasoning</li><li>Understanding of student backgrounds and interests</li><li>Opportunities for students to talk about themselves (in relation to the content)</li></ul>	<ul><li>Sarcasm or criticism of students</li><li>Disengaged students</li><li>Low expectations for students</li><li>Only the teacher talking about the content or activity</li></ul>

Figure 3.1: Instructional-snapshot document example.

Lagging Indicators

A school can identify and monitor a lagging indicator for leading indicator 2.1 by creating teacher best-practice portfolios in which teachers collect two or three artifacts of their best practices for different elements of the school's instructional model. The school can collect and archive the portfolios in digital folders that all teachers may access so they might learn from their colleagues.

Other lagging indicators that address leading indicator 2.1 include:

- The school has a written document in place that articulates the schoolwide model of instruction.

- The school provides professional development opportunities for new teachers regarding the schoolwide model of instruction.

- When asked, teachers can describe the major elements of the schoolwide model of instruction.

Quick Data and Continuous Improvement

To collect and analyze quick data for this indicator, a school could, for example, have administrators conduct periodic student focus groups. Each administrator randomly selects eight to ten students and asks them what specific instructional activities teachers currently use in different classes. The administrators do not ask students to talk about specific teachers but rather ask them to think about different activities they do in class to help them learn. The administrators then categorize these activities under specific elements in the school's instructional model.

Other examples of quick data include the following.

- Student surveys indicate teachers use specific classroom practices from the school's instructional model.

- When asked, teachers can reference specific areas of instruction they use from the school's instructional model.

- Walkthrough observation data clearly reflect practices from the school's instructional model.

Leader Accountability

Leader accountability for this indicator involves monitoring whether programs and practices are in place that lead to implementation of a schoolwide language or model of instruction and that these programs and practices are having their desired effects. Leaders can evaluate their effectiveness using the proficiency scale in figure 3.2.

Sustaining	Applying	Developing	Beginning	Not Attempting
The school continually cultivates information through quick data sources to monitor the extent to which the schoolwide language or model of instruction is consistently used, and it takes proper actions to intervene when quick data indicate a potential problem.	The school has implemented a schoolwide language or model of instruction, and it can produce lagging indicators to show the desired effects of these actions.	The school has implemented a schoolwide language or model of instruction.	The school is in the beginning, yet incomplete, stages of implementing a schoolwide language or model of instruction.	The school has not attempted to implement a schoolwide language or model of instruction.

Figure 3.2: Scale for leading indicator 2.1—The school communicates a clear vision as to how teachers should address instruction.

Leaders face challenges as they move through this scale if they do not implement an instructional model but rather simply list a set of teaching strategies or practices that have no connecting structure. As mentioned previously, leaders may face a challenge if they provide teachers with their instructional model as a digital document instead of as a hard-copy document, simply because teachers can easily forget about or ignore a digital document.

Once school leaders have established an instructional model, they should ensure the way everyone talks about instructional practices in the building reflects it. Stated negatively, if an instructional model is put in place but school leaders don't continuously use that common language themselves, then the model will not assimilate into the school's culture.

Leading Indicator 2.2

The school supports teachers to continually enhance their pedagogical skills through reflection and professional growth plans.

The Wallace Foundation Learning From Leadership Project (Louis et al., 2010) identifies a principal's ability to "empower teachers to learn and grow according to the [instructional] vision established for the school" (p. 86) as a defining characteristic of principals deemed *high performing* relative to instructional leadership. This leading indicator is specifically about creating opportunities for teachers to differentiate their own professional development based on specific aspects of instructional practice within the school's model of instruction.

To understand this approach and cultivate effective teaching practices, we find it useful to consider the hierarchy of data types in figure 3.3.

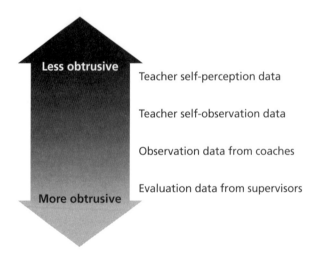

Source: Marzano Research, 2016.

Figure 3.3: Hierarchy of data types.

These data types range from very unobtrusive at the top to obtrusive at the bottom. Each data source in the hierarchy plays a key role in cultivating effective teaching in every classroom. Leading indicator 2.2 focuses clearly on the least obtrusive data types and asks teachers to assume a growth mindset regarding their own professional practice.

School leaders in this endeavor must encourage teachers to take risks and set growth goals that will grow their practice. For this purpose, consider Tom Senninger's learning zone model, shown in figure 3.4.

Panic Zone Goals	Goals set in this zone can limit personal development because they represent a potential reach too far in personal growth. Emotions associated with this zone include: Anxious, Tense, Stressed, Disinclined, Fearful
Stretch Zone Goals	Goals set in this zone offer the ideal opportunity for personal development. Emotions associated with this zone include: Excited, Anticipatory, Challenged, Expectant
Comfort Zone Goals	Goals set in this zone offer little to no personal development. This zone represents areas in which individuals are already competent and setting the goal is simply a matter of compliance. Emotions associated with this zone include: Safe, Easy, Bored, Unchallenged

Source: Adapted from © 2000 by Senniger.

Figure 3.4: Learning zone model.

Too often, people focus on goals that lie in their comfort zone because they know they will have success. Setting a goal within one's comfort zone may comply with the act of goal setting, but it does not offer much opportunity for growth because people already have skill in the selected area. For example, a teacher who can skillfully build and maintain relationships with students does not make substantial pedagogical progress if she or he sets a goal to improve in that area.

People can also reach too far in setting a goal. An overreach might take them to their panic zone and cause them to eventually abandon their goal or never truly pursue it. For example, a teacher who does not feel comfortable using technology might overreach by setting a goal to master a specific teaching technology he or she knows nothing about. Although such intent is admirable, it may produce debilitating frustrations when the teacher makes little or no progress.

Ideally, teachers should set their goals in the stretch zone. In general, the learner should find learning goals challenging yet attainable (Hattie, 2009). Goals set in a person's stretch zone should meet this criterion by offering an attainable learning challenge. Key to this indicator, school leaders must create conditions in which teachers willingly take risks and set goals that move them to their individual stretch zones so they can engage in deliberate practice for professional growth.

In the book *Becoming a Reflective Teacher*, Marzano (2012) indicates that deliberate practice involves improvement over time and that individuals engaged in deliberate practice "strive to continuously achieve mastery" (p. 7). To encourage teachers to engage in deliberate practice, school administrators need to clearly communicate that they expect teachers to take risks and experience struggles as they try new aspects of practice.

A successful leadership strategy for this purpose is to make teachers' specific growth goal areas invisible from any evaluation standpoint during a specific time period, such as the first semester. For example, if a teacher has set a goal to increase the use of physical movement for student engagement, then school leaders do not score that practice for evaluation during the first semester. Leaders make all other aspects of the teacher's practice available for evaluation, but they leave out the use of physical movement to encourage teacher growth and development in this area.

School leaders should also create opportunities that keep teachers' growth goals in the forefront of conscious practice. Too often, teachers set goals and then marginalize and eventually forget them. For a goal to progress and improve practice, it must remain a central part of a teacher's instructional focus. Several leadership strategies work well for this purpose. For instance, having teachers track their own professional growth for each goal helps teachers progress in their goals.

Figure 3.5 shows an example of a teacher's growth goal tracker from Prairie Vale Elementary in the Deer Creek School District in Oklahoma. Teachers set goals within the district instructional model and then regularly track their own progress toward improvement. Having teachers post their specific growth goals in their classroom also helps keep professional goals front and center in practice; this way, administrators, other staff, and students can see the growth goals and support teachers in their work toward their goals.

Lagging Indicators

A school can identify and monitor a lagging indicator for leading indicator 2.2 by having collaborative team members periodically discuss their growth goals in their team meetings. Each teacher takes two minutes to share and discuss his or her perceptions regarding each pedagogical growth goal. Teachers can summarize these discussions in a collaboration log and submit it to school leaders so they can monitor team members' growth goals schoolwide. Administrators and teachers set growth goals for teachers' participation in these activities. Criterion scores for this lagging indicator might focus on the percentage of teachers reporting growth.

Rate Myself Toward My Personal Goal			
4			
3.5			
3			
2.5			
2			
1.5			
1			
0.5			
0			
	Date:	Date:	Date:	Date:

What strategies have I implemented to help me reach my goal? (Date: _____)

_____

_____

What strategies have I implemented to help me reach my goal? (Date: _____)

_____

_____

How do I feel now that I meet my goal and what strategies will I continue to use in my classroom?

_____

_____

_____

_____

Source: Adapted from © 2015 by Prairie Vale Elementary.

Figure 3.5: Growth goal folder.

Other lagging indicators that address leading indicator 2.2 include:

- Teachers have written statements of their pedagogical growth goals.
- Teachers keep track of their progress on their pedagogical growth goals.
- Collaborative team leaders create a written record showing the growth goals selected by all teachers in the school.

Quick Data and Continuous Improvement

To collect and analyze quick data for this indicator, a school could, for example, create portfolios in which teachers keep three current examples of what they consider their best practices to date, relative to their specific growth goals. Teachers can keep their portfolios in digital folders that the school leader can easily access to review teachers' growth.

Other examples of quick data include the following.

- When asked, teachers can identify their specific pedagogical growth goals.
- When asked, teachers can describe their progress on their pedagogical growth goals.
- When asked, teachers can explain how they selected their pedagogical growth goals.

Leader Accountability

Leader accountability for this indicator involves monitoring whether programs and practices are in place that lead to teachers establishing growth goals for pedagogical skills and tracking their individual progress and that these programs and practices are having their desired effects. Leaders can evaluate their effectiveness using the proficiency scale in figure 3.6.

Sustaining	Applying	Developing	Beginning	Not Attempting
The school continually cultivates information through quick data sources to monitor the extent to which all teachers establish growth goals for pedagogical skills and track their individual progress, and it takes proper actions to intervene when quick data indicate a potential problem.	The school has protocols and practices in place to ensure that all teachers establish growth goals for pedagogical skills and track their individual progress, and it can produce lagging indicators to show the desired effects of these actions.	The school has protocols and practices in place to ensure that all teachers establish growth goals for pedagogical skills and track their individual progress.	The school is in the beginning, yet incomplete, stages of drafting protocols and practices to ensure that all teachers establish growth goals for pedagogical skills and track their individual progress.	The school has not attempted to ensure that all teachers establish growth goals for pedagogical skills and track their individual progress.

Figure 3.6: Scale for leading indicator 2.2—The school supports teachers to continually enhance their pedagogical skills through reflection and professional growth plans.

Leaders face challenges as they move through this scale if they do not have formal systems in place that allow teachers to track their own progress. These systems include specific checkpoint dates and self-tracking systems. If schools do not have these in place, some teachers tend to forget their growth goals as the year progresses.

Allowing teachers to set goals outside their stretch zone also poses a challenge with this indicator. Too often, the goal-setting process for personal improvement devolves into an exercise in compliance rather than in true individual professional growth. Monitoring goals from the beginning to ensure they fall into the stretch zone makes this practice more deliberate and effective.

Leading Indicator 2.3

The school is aware of and monitors predominant instructional practices.

This leading indicator is designed to provide school leaders and teachers with transparent data regarding the aggregate instructional practices within a school. In many schools, administrators already conduct walkthrough observations of instructional practices. Commonly, leaders use these walkthrough observations to provide feedback to teachers about observed instructional practices. To enact this leading indicator, principals must take one further step in the observation process. That step establishes a system that captures and organizes the collective data from walkthroughs so leaders know the predominant instructional practices across the school. Leaders do not need to identify specific teachers in these observational data; this indicator calls for knowledge of practices across the whole school, not necessarily identification of individual teachers.

Additionally, observational data should have a high level of transparency so school administrators and teachers can view or review them anytime. School administrators need to periodically review these data and let them tell the story about what is and is not happening across the school. For example, if clear communication of learning goals is a key aspect of the school's instructional model, leaders should clearly see that practice in all classrooms. If during a review of the aggregate data, administrators do not see regular, clear communication of learning goals, they should react to those data and re-engage their staff in pursuit of that practice. Likewise, if desired instructional practices persistently surface across the school, administrators should acknowledge them.

This observation and monitoring practice should be continuous throughout the school year but organized for viewing in specific chunks of time to reveal data that school leaders can act on immediately. Leaders should think of this practice as "chapters in a book." By collecting this data in specific time-sequenced periods, they can enact ongoing monitoring of the predominant practices and react to the data as needed. The strength in monitoring this way is the ability to see the need for interventions to recommit to specific instructional practices schoolwide or to celebrate the use of specific instructional practices schoolwide.

Setting up a system for periodic review provides ongoing monitoring and allows leaders to know if the predominant practices that were not occurring in September are actually improving in October, or if predominant practices tend to fall off and not be as evident during specific months or time periods. If the data is simply organized as one ongoing data set, it becomes nearly impossible to determine the predominant practices and when they actually occurred or if they are presently occurring. Eventually, the combined data sets will tell the story for the entire school year and serve as a reflective assessment for the year instructionally. Collective data sets can provide a good basis for planning and revisiting instructional practices with the entire staff.

Transparency in this data is extremely useful. For example, a principal might be able to use the data to show how during the initial two weeks of December, nearly all specific instructional strategies saw a decline in usage as compared to the first three months of the school year. This could lead to a strategic discussion about why that occurred and what the school can do to keep from losing this type of instructional time in the future.

Figure 3.7 shows an example of this practice from Epperly Elementary in Midwest City, Oklahoma, which uses a predominant practices board.

This board hangs in the teacher workroom so anyone can openly view it at any time. The principal and assistant principal use tally marks to indicate which practices they observe as they conduct classroom walkthroughs. Periodically, they take a picture of the board for their archive copy of that time period and then erase the board and populate it with new observational data so the data are current and allow for ongoing monitoring of predominant practices.

Lagging Indicators

A school can identify and monitor a lagging indicator for leading indicator 2.3 by creating a PowerPoint presentation for the staff each month that shares what leaders aggregately do or do not observe from the school's instructional model. Each month, it adds a new slide to the presentation so the staff as a whole can see the progression or consistency of predominant instructional practices occurring in the school. Leaders set criterion goals in terms of the frequency of use of specific practices. For example, a principal might set a criterion goal such as the following: 95 percent of all teachers will be observed communicating clear learning goals each month. This provides a target expectation for the staff and gives the principal data he or she can communicate to the staff to immediately correct a lack of this practice or celebrate each time the criterion goal is achieved throughout the school year.

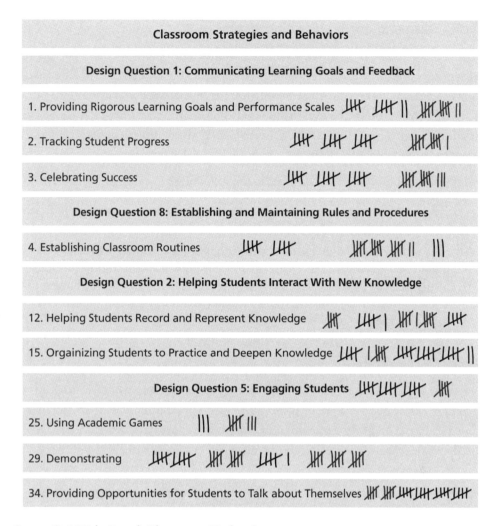

Source: © 2015 by Epperly Elementary. Used with permission.

Figure 3.7: Instructional strategy tracker.

Other lagging indicators that address leading indicator 2.3 include:

- Administrators put in place a system of tracking aggregate classroom walkthrough data and periodically update and review the data throughout the school year.

- Staff meeting agendas or artifacts indicate school leaders share the predominant practice information with their staff.

- School leaders can clearly identify the predominant practices across the entire school and the instructional practices they do not see used predominantly.

Quick Data and Continuous Improvement

To collect and analyze quick data for this indicator, a school could, for example, have leadership team members take pictures and short videos of specific instructional practices observed during walkthroughs or extended classroom evaluations. Each administrator on the leadership team then shares his or her pictures or videos at administrative meetings so the team can collectively monitor what instructional practices occur across the school.

Other examples of quick data include the following.

- The school leader audits random teacher evaluation documents to look for patterns of using specific instructional practices.

- The school leader uses focused walkthrough visits, during which several members of a school team split up and do quick walkthroughs in as many classrooms as possible in a compacted time (such as forty-five minutes) to look for certain instructional practices, such as clear communication of learning goals.

Leader Accountability

Leader accountability for this indicator involves monitoring whether programs and practices are in place that lead to monitoring the predominant schoolwide instructional strategies and that these programs and practices are having their desired effects. Leaders can evaluate their effectiveness using the proficiency scale in figure 3.8.

Sustaining	Applying	Developing	Beginning	Not Attempting
The school continually cultivates information through quick data sources to monitor the predominant schoolwide instructional practices, and it takes proper actions to intervene when quick data indicate a potential problem.	The school has protocols and practices in place to monitor the predominant schoolwide instructional strategies, and it can produce lagging indicators to show the desired effects of these actions.	The school has protocols and practices in place to monitor the predominant schoolwide instructional strategies.	The school is in the beginning, yet incomplete, stages of drafting protocols and practices to monitor the predominant schoolwide instructional strategies.	The school has not attempted to monitor the predominant schoolwide instructional strategies.

Figure 3.8: Scale for leading indicator 2.3—The school is aware of and monitors predominant instructional practices.

Leaders face challenges as they move through this scale if they do not establish a simple monitoring system that allows them to depict the differences in instructional practices that occur in different observation periods. If the system does not allow leaders to monitor instruction in small chunks over time, it becomes difficult to document which practices occur currently and which may have occurred two months prior. School leaders need to remember to wipe the slate clean for analysis at each observation period so they know if the predominant practices in October are the same as those in February.

Having transparency with staff on what leaders observe across the school also poses a challenge. Because these data are not personalized, leaders should display them openly. This way, staff can continually monitor themselves and compare and contrast the aggregate data with their own predominant practices.

Leading Indicator 2.4

The school provides teachers with clear, ongoing evaluations of their pedagogical strengths and weaknesses that are based on multiple sources of data and are consistent with student achievement data.

Teacher evaluation is a complex topic, especially since the advent of Race to the Top (RTT) legislation. Specifically, in July 2009, President Barack Obama and Secretary of Education Arne Duncan announced the RTT initiative with an overall budget of about $4.35 billion. The program offered states significant funding if they were willing to develop and implement more rigorous and comprehensive systems to evaluate teachers and principals. As stated in the U.S. Department of Education's (2010) *A Blueprint for Reform*, RTT had the following priority:

> We will elevate the teaching profession to focus on recognizing, encouraging, and rewarding excellence. We are calling on states and districts to develop and implement systems of teacher and principal evaluation and support, and to identify effective and highly effective teachers and principals on the basis of student growth and other factors. (p. 4)

The impetus for RTT, at least in part, came from two high-visibility reports: *Rush to Judgment* (Toch & Rothman, 2008) and *The Widget Effect* (Weisberg, Sexton, Mulhern, & Keeling, 2009). Taken together, they find that even in school systems in which students continually do not demonstrate adequate growth in learning, teachers still have high evaluations. For example, Daniel Weisberg, Susan Sexton, Jennifer Mulhern, and David Keeling (2009) found that within one large district, 87 percent of the six hundred schools did not give a single unsatisfactory rating to their teachers even though more than 10 percent of those schools had been classified by the state as failing educationally. In all, only 0.3 percent of the district's teachers received *unsatisfactory* ratings, but 93 percent of the teachers received *excellent* or *superior* ratings. Clearly, RTT was designed to create an education system that more accurately differentiates between effective and ineffective teachers so schools can provide the necessary supports to take corrective actions.

Unfortunately, not a great deal has changed in terms of the distribution of teaching ratings (Kraft & Gilmour, 2017). Even after all this money and energy spent, teacher evaluation systems still do not differentiate well between high-performing and low-performing teachers.

One reason for this is that when schools use instructional models designed for teacher development for the purposes of teacher evaluation, they do not set aside enough time for teacher observation. To illustrate, reconsider the instructional model we introduced in the section on leading indicator 2.1 (see page 78). It contains forty-three elements, each with multiple embedded instructional strategies. Robert Marzano and Michael D. Toth (2013) estimate that it takes upwards of ten observations to accurately assess a teacher in all the elements. Unfortunately, administrators typically only have time for two or three observations.

Research indicates that when administrators do not have enough time to make accurate observations, they tend to err on the side of giving teachers high observation scores (Kraft & Gilmour, 2017). For this reason, we propose that administrators use the ten categories in table 3.2 for observations focused on teacher evaluation.

Table 3.2: Ten Categories for Teacher Evaluation

	Teacher Actions	Student Mental States and Processes
Feedback	Providing and Communicating Clear Learning Goals	1. Students understand the progression of knowledge they are expected to master and where they are along that progression.
	Using Assessments	2. Students understand how test scores and grades relate to their status on the progression of knowledge they are expected to master.
Content	Conducting Direct Instruction Lessons	3. When content is new, students understand which parts are important and how the parts fit together.
	Conducting Practicing and Deepening Lessons	4. After teachers present new content, students deepen their understanding and develop fluency in skills and processes.
	Conducting Knowledge Application Lessons	5. After teachers present new content, students generate and defend claims through knowledge application tasks.
	Using Strategies That Appear in All Types of Lessons	6. Students continually integrate new knowledge with old knowledge and revise their understanding accordingly.

	Teacher Actions	Student Mental States and Processes
Context	Using Engagement Strategies	7. Students are paying attention, energized, intrigued, and inspired.
	Implementing Rules and Procedures	8. Students understand and follow rules and procedures.
	Building Relationships	9. Students feel welcome, accepted, and valued.
	Communicating High Expectations	10. Typically reluctant students feel valued and do not hesitate to interact with the teacher or their peers.

Source: Marzano, 2017, pp. 5–6.

Leaders can quite accurately observe behaviors described in the right column of table 3.2 with a small set of observations. For example, observers can typically score teachers quite accurately on the ten sets of behaviors in table 3.2 with only three observations. Additionally, leaders can supplement the teacher observation process in a few ways, including by taking video submissions. With time availability representing one of the biggest hurdles to gathering multiple data points for evaluation, it stands to reason that administrators, as evaluators, could effectively use video recordings of teacher practice in combination with live classroom observations. Recordings allow evaluators to observe instruction during times that work well in their schedule, and they offer them the opportunity to review the instruction multiple times for better accuracy in what they see and hear. Using video also provides a very fair opportunity for teachers to select the videos they submit. This allows teachers to work at getting the best video they can possibly submit, which, in turn, means they improve instruction as they strive for a video of outstanding practice.

Evaluators should not conduct observations uniformly across all teachers. Instead, they need to deploy their time where teachers need it most in order to address the different needs and levels of teacher growth in their school. For this reason, leaders should consider dividing the teaching staff into three specific tiers for evaluation purposes.

- **Tier one:** These are the most effective teachers. Leaders have great confidence in these teachers' instructional practices, and these teachers have shown consistency in the use of effective practice. Leaders should observe these teachers about once each month to provide feedback and look for continued effective practices.

- **Tier two:** These teachers do a good job yet have areas in which leaders would like to see improvement. This category typically includes the most teachers. Leaders should observe these teachers twice each month and have preparations in place to move them to tier one if they show significant improvement.

- **Tier three:** These teachers need improvement, or they and their students are at risk of losing ground. This group should get extra attention in the form of evaluation so evaluators can grow these teachers' skills or clearly decide whether these teachers will meet the school's instructional expectations.

Leaders should observe these teachers once each week, staggering the length of observations to meet the specific needs of each teacher. For example, if a teacher is having a difficult time starting class, an observer might engage in a short visit at the beginning of class.

By establishing evaluation tiers, administrators can more effectively allocate evaluation time where teachers need it most. Teachers do not need to know which tier they appear in for evaluation purposes. Administrators should periodically reflect on different teachers who show progress and may need to move to a higher tier, and teachers who show signs in their practice that might warrant movement to a lower tier.

For this leading indicator, administrators should consider that teacher evaluations must have consistency with student achievement data. This does not mean they should use student achievement data as a measure for teacher evaluation. Instead, the data should serve as checks and balances for administrators to see if their evaluation results correlate to student data trends. For example, if 90 percent of the teachers in a school rank as *high performing*, then student data should show trends of growth and improvement in student learning. However, given the same teacher evaluation results, if a school's student achievement data have dropped or show little or no growth, then the results do not accurately represent something, most often the quality of teaching occurring in classrooms.

Lagging Indicators

A school can identify and monitor a lagging indicator for leading indicator 2.4 by assigning each teacher to one of the three teacher tiers at the beginning of the school year, and then assigning each to a tier again at the end of the first semester and the end of the year before writing summative evaluations. At each checkpoint, administrators note which teachers should move tiers, and the administrative team discusses the specific evaluation data that inform teachers' movements to different tiers. The team sets quantitative goals for and monitors teacher movement through the tiers.

Other lagging indicators that address leading indicator 2.4 include:

- School leaders ensure that highly specific rubrics are in place to provide teachers with accurate feedback on their pedagogical strengths and weaknesses.

- Administrators base teacher feedback and evaluation data on multiple sources of information, including but not limited to direct observation, teacher self-reports, and analysis of teacher performance captured on video.

- The school leader has a schedule indicating frequent observations and feedback to teachers.

Quick Data and Continuous Improvement

To collect and analyze quick data for this indicator, a school could, for example, have each administrator report monthly on whom and what they have observed during teacher evaluations for the past month. Each administrator reports on how many evaluations he or she did that month and what he or she observed from each teacher that month.

Other examples of quick data include the following.

- When asked, teachers can describe their most recent teacher evaluation data.
- Teachers can identify multiple times when evaluators have evaluated them.
- When asked, evaluators can explain the variety of strategies they use for teacher evaluation.

Leader Accountability

Leader accountability for this indicator involves monitoring whether programs and practices are in place that lead to specific evaluation data for teachers regarding pedagogical strengths and weaknesses and that these programs and practices are having their desired effects. Leaders can evaluate their effectiveness using the proficiency scale in figure 3.9 (page 96).

Challenges leaders face as they move through the levels of this scale include administrators not scheduling time for teacher evaluation on their calendars well in advance. As a best practice, they should block out specific chunks of time each week designated for teacher evaluation. When they do not have this practice in place, administrators quickly lose potential evaluation time to a host of other issues, and that results in fewer evaluations or evaluations conducted more as an act of compliance than as an act of timely feedback and growth.

Another challenge arises when administrators do not know the school's instructional model well enough to recognize specific elements and strategies in the classroom. To become effective evaluators of instruction, administrators must possess a clear understanding of the pedagogical techniques they observe.

Sustaining	Applying	Developing	Beginning	Not Attempting
The school continually cultivates information through quick data sources to monitor the collection of specific evaluation data for each teacher regarding pedagogical strengths and weaknesses and that these data are gathered from multiple sources, and it takes proper actions to intervene when quick data indicate a potential problem.	The school has protocols and practices in place to ensure that specific evaluation data are collected for each teacher regarding pedagogical strengths and weaknesses and that these data are gathered from multiple sources, and it can produce lagging indicators to show the desired effects of these actions.	The school has protocols and practices in place to ensure that specific evaluation data are collected for each teacher regarding pedagogical strengths and weaknesses and that these data are gathered from multiple sources.	The school is in the beginning, yet incomplete, stages of drafting protocols and practices to ensure that specific evaluation data are collected for each teacher regarding pedagogical strengths and weaknesses and that these data are gathered from multiple sources.	The school has not attempted to ensure that specific evaluation data are collected for each teacher regarding pedagogical strengths and weaknesses and that these data are gathered from multiple sources.

Figure 3.9: Scale for leading indicator 2.4—The school provides teachers with clear, ongoing evaluations of their pedagogical strengths and weaknesses that are based on multiple sources of data and are consistent with student achievement data.

Leading Indicator 2.5

The school provides teachers with job-embedded professional development that is directly related to their instructional growth goals.

Marzano, Frontier, and Livingston (2011) emphasize that schools have not traditionally differentiated professional development opportunities to address teachers' personal development as professional learners. Instead, schools have often approached professional development with a one-size-fits-all strategy. This leading indicator deals with schools differentiating to meet teachers' individual needs as professional learners. This indicator directly connects to leading indicator 2.2 and the professional goals teachers identify for their own practice. Schools often use the term *job-embedded professional development*, but they do not often practice this development. To implement this leading indicator, school leaders need to identify and establish tools and structures that engage teachers in job-embedded professional development. Some of those tools include (1) instructional coaching, (2) instructional video library, and (3) video reflection.

1. **Instructional coaching:** Instructional coaching represents one of the most effective job-embedded professional development tools available to school leaders. When they implement it for this purpose, instructional coaches focus their efforts on the growth goals individual teachers identify. Rather than providing instructional coaching over a broad spectrum of instructional practices, coaches focus on growing thin slices of excellence within each teacher's practice based on the goals each teacher identifies. This approach offers coaches an opportunity to provide explicit feedback to teachers as they focus on gradually growing specific practices. For this purpose, coaches should use a rubric that identifies increments of teacher growth over time. In the book *Coaching Classroom Instruction*, Robert Marzano and Julia A. Simms (2013) provide a coaching rubric, shown in figure 3.10, that coaches can use to observe and provide coaching feedback for almost any instructional practice a teacher works on.

4 Innovating	3 Applying	2 Developing	1 Beginning	0 Not Using
The teacher integrates several strategies to create a macrostrategy or adapts strategies for unique student needs and situations.	The teacher uses strategies or behaviors associated with an element and monitors their effects on student outcomes.	The teacher uses strategies or behaviors associated with an element, but in a mechanistic way.	The teacher uses strategies or behaviors associated with an element incorrectly or with parts missing.	The teacher is unaware of strategies or behaviors associated with an element.

Source: Marzano & Simms, 2013, p. 23.

Figure 3.10: Generic rubric for classroom instruction.

2. **Instructional video library:** Using video for job-embedded professional development can provide teachers with several options to help grow their individual practices. Schools can establish a video library of teaching practices and code the instructional videos based on the school's instructional model, identifying them by instructional strategy. Teachers can view examples of quality practice to gain ideas for specific areas they have identified in their growth goals.

3. **Video reflection:** Teachers can also record and review their own practice for self-improvement as part of job-embedded professional development. With existing technologies, this practice becomes quite easy. For example, using

smartphones or iPads, teachers record themselves as they implement strategies based on their own growth goals and review the video themselves or with instructional coaches. The practice of self-review through video holds great potential for individual professional growth but, to date, remains underutilized.

In his book *The Tipping Point: How Little Things Can Make a Big Difference*, Malcolm Gladwell (2002) describes how a few people can cause an idea to grow from small to big. These people, called *connectors*, have the ability to come in contact with and influence a large number of people. School leaders should identify key teacher leaders who are willing to try this practice and share their thoughts about the experience with their colleagues. We have coached several principals to use this strategy with connector teachers as they begin implementation of personal video review. In nearly every case, these connector teachers have made the same comments about their video reflections. They commented on how they don't like their recorded voice, but they can see numerous things in their practice that provide them with valuable ideas for their own growth. As additional teachers engage in personal video review, this practice hits the tipping point and becomes a very cost-effective system for job-embedded professional development.

Lagging Indicators

A school can identify and monitor a lagging indicator for leading indicator 2.5 by having teachers record specific areas of instruction on video and then meet with an instructional coach or administrator to watch the video together and discuss what went well and natural next steps for growth. Each teacher records his or her practice once each semester and reviews the video. Leaders keep records and establish goals as to the number and quality of such interactions with teachers.

Other lagging indicators that address leading indicator 2.5 include:

- Teachers have online professional development resources available to them regarding their instructional growth goals.
- Teachers have teacher-led professional development available to them regarding their instructional growth goals.
- Teachers have instructional coaching available to them regarding their instructional growth goals.

Quick Data and Continuous Improvement

To collect and analyze quick data for this indicator, a school could, for example, put QR codes in the staff workroom that link to a quick survey. The survey asks teachers to identify the different aspects of job-embedded professional development they have been involved in during the school year. Leaders then review these quick survey data to determine which aspects of job-embedded professional development their staff use consistently and continuously.

Other examples of quick data include the following.

- When asked, teachers can describe specific practices they are trying as a result of their job-embedded professional development.
- When asked, teachers can describe how professional development supports their attainment of instructional growth goals.
- Instructional coaches can identify the specific strategies they use to grow individual teacher practice in coordination with teachers' growth goals.

Leader Accountability

Leader accountability for this indicator involves monitoring whether programs and practices are in place that lead to job-embedded professional development directly related to teachers' instructional growth goals and that these programs and practices are having their desired effects. Leaders can evaluate their effectiveness using the proficiency scale in figure 3.11.

Sustaining	Applying	Developing	Beginning	Not Attempting
The school continually cultivates information through quick data sources to monitor job-embedded professional development directly related to teachers' instructional growth goals, and it takes proper actions to intervene when quick data indicate a potential problem.	The school has protocols and practices in place to ensure that job-embedded professional development directly related to teachers' instructional growth goals is provided, and it can produce lagging indicators to show the desired effects of these actions.	The school has protocols and practices in place to ensure that job-embedded professional development directly related to teachers' instructional growth goals is provided.	The school is in the beginning, yet incomplete, stages of drafting protocols and practices to ensure that job-embedded professional development directly related to teachers' instructional growth goals is provided.	The school has not attempted to ensure that job-embedded professional development directly related to teachers' instructional growth goals is provided.

Figure 3.11: Scale for leading indicator 2.5—The school provides teachers with job-embedded professional development that is directly related to their instructional growth goals.

Leaders face challenges as they move through this scale if they do not establish a clear distinction between instructional coaching and evaluation. Teachers need to see coaching as a growth opportunity in which they go through different stages of growth as they add new aspects to their practice.

If a school has an absence of available instructional coaches, it is imperative that school leaders establish other systems that offer job-embedded professional development. Virtual systems can help with this aspect. For example, the Marzano Compendium of Instructional Strategies (www.marzanoresearch.com) provides video-based professional development, including ten categories of instructional elements; each of the forty-three elements has a number of strategies associated with it.

Administrators must ensure that job-embedded professional development focuses on each teacher's specific growth goals, which promotes differentiation for teachers as professional learners.

Leading Indicator 2.6

Teachers have opportunities to observe and discuss effective teaching.

The key to this leading indicator is not only observing effective instruction but also debriefing those observations. This process has the potential to expand individual teacher practice schoolwide and cultivate collaboration regarding instructional practice. School leaders can enact this leading indicator through the implementation of both live and virtual instructional rounds.

Whereas schools use several versions of instructional rounds, we use the instructional rounds model developed by Marzano (2011) because of its focus on teacher development. This model does not intend in any way to evaluate the teachers under observation; rather, it intends to give teachers an opportunity to gain ideas for their own professional practice through observing colleagues. During instructional rounds, teachers visit the classrooms of other teachers, not to critique or evaluate them, but to observe similarities and differences between how they employ instructional strategies and how the teachers they observe employ instructional strategies. We advise that administrators not participate in instructional rounds, because we have found that when administrators participate in rounds, teachers interpret the observations as evaluative.

However, administrators play critical roles in the logistics and operation of instructional rounds. They identify the teachers to observe during the instructional rounds. If the purpose of rounds is for teachers to gain ideas for their own practice, then the teachers under observation should be those who regularly display the instructional practices school leaders would like to see replicated across their schools. Ideally, a school would have the ability to say that every teacher on its campus has rounds-worthy classroom practices to observe. But in reality, that is not always the case, so administrators must take on the key role of identifying the teachers to observe.

In our model of instructional rounds, a small group of three to five teachers, including the rounds leader, observes another teacher for ten to fifteen minutes. While doing so, the group members consider and record information on three key reflection questions.

1. What do I see and hear that reaffirms something I do?
2. What do I see and hear that I would like to know more about?
3. What do I see and hear that I would like to try in my own practice immediately?

The power of these three questions comes from their inward focus on the observers' growth, not from an external focus on the observed teacher.

Following the observation, teachers who participate in the rounds have a few minutes to collect their thoughts for discussion. Then the rounds leader uses the three questions and conducts a debrief discussion with the group, sharing his or her observations and thoughts. This debrief often opens the door for instructional coaching opportunities when teachers discuss instructional strategies they would like to know more about or try in their own practice. Because of the close link to instructional coaching, leading instructional rounds is a productive practice for instructional coaches as part of their role in cultivating effective teaching in every classroom.

Whether to give feedback to teachers observed on the rounds is a school-based decision. If a school decides to offer feedback from the rounds to teachers, the feedback should come from the rounds leader and cover the effective practices the group observed while in the classroom. Often, the rounds leader can put this feedback in an email format and send it directly to the teacher following the rounds debriefing session. Figure 3.12 shows an example of this kind of email.

We learned so many things from observing you during the instructional round yesterday!

Here are some of the amazing practices we saw in your double-block algebra classroom that we want to incorporate into our own learning.

- **Constant assessment of student progress:** You rotated continually among the student tables, checking for understanding and correcting misconceptions.
- **Peer teaching:** We heard students teaching each other and engaging in "math talk."
- **Your "If you are not sure, ask a question" poster:** We liked that you give students a visual reminder that it is OK to seek information.
- **A warm and inviting classroom:** This is a mathematics class we all would like to take!

Figure 3.12: Example instructional rounds feedback email.

Lagging Indicators

A school can identify and monitor a lagging indicator for leading indicator 2.6 by creating a digital instructional rounds calendar that identifies the different days each month for conducting rounds. The school asks teachers to sign up for one specific time each semester to participate in rounds on a first-come, first-serve basis. Leaders can use the digital tool to quantify and analyze the frequency of rounds, and criterion scores would focus on the percentage of teachers who participate in rounds.

Other lagging indicators that address leading indicator 2.6 include:

- Teachers have opportunities to engage in instructional rounds.
- Teachers have opportunities to view and discuss video-based examples of exemplary teaching.
- Teachers have regular times to meet and discuss effective instructional practices (for example, lesson studies).

Quick Data and Continuous Improvement

To collect and analyze quick data for this indicator, a school could, for example, have the rounds group members chart how frequently they observe different aspects of the school's instructional model using dots on chart paper coded with the school's instructional elements. At the end of the debriefing session, the rounds group quickly places sticky dots by each instructional element it just saw and discussed. This chart helps the administrative team quickly see what specific instructional aspects the group observed and discussed in each debriefing session.

Other examples of quick data include the following.

- When asked, teachers can describe ideas they have tried in their own practice as a result of instructional rounds or videos of effective teaching they have observed.
- School leaders make information available regarding teacher participation in instructional rounds.
- Instructional rounds leaders provide brief summaries of teacher discussion points following instructional rounds.

Leader Accountability

Leader accountability for this indicator involves monitoring whether programs and practices are in place that lead to teachers having opportunities to observe and discuss effective teaching virtually or in person and that these programs and practices are having their desired effects. Leaders can evaluate their effectiveness using the proficiency scale in figure 3.13.

Sustaining	Applying	Developing	Beginning	Not Attempting
The school continually cultivates information through quick data sources to monitor teachers' opportunities to observe and discuss effective teaching virtually or in person, and it takes proper actions to intervene when quick data indicate a potential problem.	The school has protocols and practices in place to ensure that teachers have opportunities to observe and discuss effective teaching virtually or in person, and it can produce lagging indicators to show the desired effects of these actions.	The school has protocols and practices in place to ensure that teachers have opportunities to observe and discuss effective teaching virtually or in person.	The school is in the beginning, yet incomplete, stages of drafting protocols and practices to ensure that teachers have opportunities to observe and discuss effective teaching virtually or in person.	The school has not attempted to ensure that teachers have opportunities to observe and discuss effective teaching virtually or in person.

Figure 3.13: Scale for leading indicator 2.6—Teachers have opportunities to observe and discuss effective teaching.

As leaders move through this scale, they may find the live instructional rounds process poses challenges in a small school. This is simply because there might not be enough teachers in a building to observe or form groups of observers. In these cases, the school can use virtual rounds in the same manner, by watching a video or two of instructional practices and following the same debriefing protocol.

Failing to make time for the debriefing session also causes a challenge. This limits the effectiveness of instructional rounds. Although the observation includes growth, more growth occurs when the rounds group debriefs and discusses what group members observed.

Not using rounds consistently can cause an issue because group members develop skills and a feel for facilitating the debriefing sessions. These skills will tend to degrade if rounds do not occur for long periods of time. If possible, a school should have a few people who serve as rounds leaders. Leading rounds is a natural extension of instructional coaching, so instructional coaches should serve as rounds leaders if possible. Leading rounds is a natural extension of instructional coaching, so instructional coaches should serve as rounds leaders.

Level 2 Transformations

From the perspective of all those variables that correlate with student achievement (see Hattie, 2009, 2012, 2015), level 2 of the HRS model deals with perhaps the most powerful alterable variable school leaders might focus on—the quality of classroom instruction. We have seen some powerful results when school leaders take this on. Following are a few examples.

Principal Cirsten Lewis of Whiteland Elementary School in Whiteland, Indiana, believes the work done at level 2 leads to a clear picture of quality instruction. Mrs. Lewis describes that work as follows:

> Our school and district's level of commitment to quality instruction has never been more urgent. Our mindset has morphed as a result. Instead of assuming that only some students can perform at high levels, we espouse the belief that *all* students can and will do so. This work will never be easy.
>
> Each year since we began on this HRS journey, we have uncovered new ways to improve our instructional practices. Conducting instructional rounds and instructional audits has been especially beneficial, for we are able to reduce our focus on teacher evaluation while increasing our focus on our most valuable stakeholders—the students.
>
> This year, utilizing *The New Art and Science of Teaching* (Marzano, 2017) has afforded us the opportunity to deeply reflect upon our practices. After receiving our instructional audit results, we set individual, team, and schoolwide professional growth plans accordingly. This book provides strategies for visualizing and planning quality instructional practices that will directly affect student learning outcomes. Instructional leaders become out of touch unless they participate in deep practice regarding teaching and learning. In my over seventeen years as an educator, I have never before had such a clear road map to success in the classroom. (C. Lewis, personal communication, September 21, 2017)

Samantha Gladwell serves as a teacher and instructional coach for NYOS (Not Your Ordinary School) Charter School in Austin, Texas. Ms. Gladwell reflects on what level 2 of the HRS model has brought to her professional life as a classroom teacher:

> Knowing that our teacher evaluation system is focused on growth encourages me to take risks and push myself instructionally. The teacher scales for reflective practice help me honestly evaluate my current skill level and set specific goals for personal development. I appreciate receiving feedback related to my goal when my administrators conduct classroom walkthroughs. (S. Gladwell, personal communication, August 21, 2017)

Bobby Kelley and Tammy Schaefer serve as the secondary principal and elementary principal respectively at Cross County Community School in Stromsburg, Nebraska. Cross County is a high-performing district that implemented several aspects of the HRS model before clearly focusing on the model in 2015. As part of their HRS work, these two principals have instituted a very successful system for instructional coaching by crossing over and serving as the instructional coaches for each other's staff. That way, teachers don't perceive them as evaluators, and they can establish a coaching relationship with teachers who are not members of the staff they evaluate. This approach has cultivated new instructional growth opportunities for their district as a whole. Here, they explain the approach's effects in their own words:

> Our district has been working with Marzano Research for the past four years, which includes the HRS program for the past two. The HRS framework has allowed us to enhance our teachers' delivery of instruction through our flipped coaching model. This systematic approach has strengthened our sense of community throughout our preK–12 district. In addition, the HRS framework has inspired a new level of excitement and enthusiasm for professional growth among our teachers. (B. Kelley and T. Schaefer, personal communication, August 8, 2017)

Conclusion

Leadership for level 2 of the HRS model focuses on effective teaching in every classroom. Such an emphasis directly addresses question 5 of the six critical questions Rick described in the introductory chapter: How will we increase our instructional competence? This level has six leading indicators. For a school to declare itself highly reliable relative to level 2, leaders must generate lagging indicators with clear criteria for success. Even after the school has met these success criteria, the school must still continue to collect quick data to monitor and react to variations in its performance on the six indicators.

Chapter 4
Guaranteed and Viable Curriculum

● ● ●

Level 3 of the HRS model is directly aligned with the first of the six critical questions Rick described in the introductory chapter: What is it we want students to learn? To answer this question precisely and efficiently, a school must develop a guaranteed and viable curriculum.

Marzano (2003) first coined the term *guaranteed and viable curriculum* in the book *What Works in Schools*. This term refers to a very simple but powerful construct. No matter who teaches a specific course or specific content at a certain grade level in a school, students should have the opportunity to learn the same content. Stated negatively, it should not be the case that students receive one curriculum for fifth-grade science from one teacher and quite another curriculum from that teacher's colleague across the hall. This represents the *guaranteed* aspect of level 3 in the HRS model. Additionally, teachers should have adequate time and resources to teach what's guaranteed. Again, stated negatively, there should not be so much guaranteed content that it makes it impossible for teachers to address it effectively. At level 3, an HRS ensures a lean and focused curriculum that addresses all essentials.

Level 3 of the HRS model has six leading indicators.

3.1 The school curriculum and accompanying assessments adhere to state and district standards.

3.2 The school curriculum is focused enough that teachers can adequately address it in the time they have available.

3.3 All students have the opportunity to learn the critical content of the curriculum.

3.4 The school establishes clear and measurable goals that are focused on critical needs regarding improving overall student achievement at the school level.

3.5 The school analyzes, interprets, and uses data to regularly monitor progress toward school achievement goals.

3.6 The school establishes appropriate school- and classroom-level programs and practices to help students meet individual achievement goals when data indicate interventions are needed.

Leading Indicator 3.1

The school curriculum and accompanying assessments adhere to state and district standards.

In the era of standards and accountability, school leaders should think about curriculum for any content using three interrelated curriculum types. The first is the *intended curriculum*, which national, state, and district standards determine. The second, the *implemented curriculum*, actually gets taught in classrooms. Students actually learn the third type, the *attained curriculum*, in each grade level or course. Ideally, these three curricula align so the intended curriculum is the implemented curriculum and the implemented curriculum is the attained curriculum. In many cases, alignment breaks down between the first and second types, and teachers do not always teach the intended.

Grant Wiggins and Jay McTighe (2007) state, "As presently written, most curricula encourage and enable teachers to do the worst possible thing: go off and work entirely on their own" (p. 38). Leadership actions for this leading indicator should help ensure the intended curriculum is, in fact, the implemented curriculum.

Teachers often refer to their textbook or a specific program when they are asked about their curriculum. They do this because their school does not have curriculum documents available, or they exist in an inefficient format. School leaders should ensure that they make curriculum documents the first and easiest documents a teacher or collaborative team can access, and these documents should drive their decision making for the initial question, What is it we want students to learn? Teachers should also first ask this question within the collaborative team process to clearly focus on the intended curriculum.

While many districts have created curriculum maps and pacing guides for this purpose, teachers should actively use and review them as they plan units of instruction. School leaders should periodically audit classroom assessments and activities to ensure they, in fact, align with the intended curriculum.

Leaders can monitor this indicator by collecting the artifacts from the work of collaborative teams. For example, if school leaders ask collaborative teams to develop common assessments as part of their PLC process, they should periodically review and audit these assessments and the results. Using a random audit approach to monitor common assessments both saves time and maintains that any team or teacher could be randomly selected for auditing at any time. This audit also allows school leaders to review the quality of the assessments given. Leaders should look for the proper level of rigor in the assessments as compared to the standards and look at the items or tasks themselves to review them for bias that might affect assessment results. The following example depicts the way an assessment audit system might work.

A principal, an assistant principal, and an instructional coach collect common assessment examples from the collaborative teams in their school. Each is assigned a group of teams from which they will collect the examples. Once each month, all three review the common assessment examples in comparison to the curriculum for the related content. As part of this process, they review the assessments' alignment to the curriculum as well as the assessment types and their quality. As a group, they provide feedback about the assessments or ask the teams or teachers reflective questions when necessary. For this purpose, each collaborative team receives a digital folder where it can post copies or explanations of its common assessments. This allows the assessment audit to occur seamlessly and allows the school leadership team easy access to monitor curriculum and assessment practices.

Using pre- and postassessments within instructional units, and tracking learners' knowledge gain on specific standards, can provide a quick data source for school leaders to ensure the intended curriculum is the implemented curriculum. Pre- and postassessment data also offer indications of the attained curriculum and where students most commonly have difficulties, which, in turn, allows school leaders to look at potential gaps in school curriculum that they might easily fix.

One such example of this involves a middle school, which was teaching particularly important seventh-grade mathematics concepts that students had to understand and use for seventh-grade physical science standards. After examining the results of its pre- and postassessments, the science team decided to ask the mathematics team if it taught a particular mathematics standard, because based on the data, incorrect mathematics was the common error among students in science. As a result of this discussion, the teams discovered that the mathematics team taught the related mathematics concepts during the six-week period after the science team had already taught the physical science standards. The teams fixed this gap simply by rearranging the curriculum so the mathematics teachers taught the related mathematics concepts *before* the science teachers presented the seventh-grade physical science standards.

Lagging Indicators

A school can identify and monitor a lagging indicator for leading indicator 3.1 by having 100 percent of the collaborative teams within the school develop and submit their scope-and-sequence documents, indicating which standards they will prioritize, the order in which they will teach them, and tentative plans for when they will teach them. Teachers can provide updates each quarter, stating where each team is in its sequence and outlining changes made along the way. Teachers can also create common assessments aligned to the priority standards and share them with the entire school in a shared digital folder. The school guiding coalition reviews all these products on a quarterly basis.

Other lagging indicators that address leading indicator 3.1 include:

- Curriculum documents are in place that correlate the written curriculum with state and district standards.

- Documents are available that examine the extent to which assessments accurately measure the written and taught curriculum.

- Curriculum maps are in place referencing the specific standards addressed during specific time frames in the school year.

Quick Data and Continuous Improvement

To collect and analyze quick data for this indicator, a school could, for example, periodically have leaders gather a couple of assessments from each grade level or teacher team and look for their connections to state and district standards. The school leadership team then compiles and shares results regarding the assessments' alignment with the whole school, and leaders provide feedback as necessary to any teams whose assessments do not have good alignment.

Other examples of quick data include the following.

- When asked, teachers can identify the specific standards they address in their lessons.

- Teachers code sample common assessments to show the standards they measure.

- When asked, teachers or teacher teams can explain how they have designed lessons to address specific standards they currently teach.

Leader Accountability

Leader accountability for this indicator involves monitoring whether programs and practices are in place that lead to the curriculum and accompanying assessments adhering to state and district standards and that these programs and practices are having their desired effects. Leaders can evaluate their effectiveness using the proficiency scale in figure 4.1.

Sustaining	Applying	Developing	Beginning	Not Attempting
The school continually cultivates information through quick data sources to monitor adherence of the school's curriculum to state and district standards, and it takes proper actions to intervene when quick data indicate a potential problem.	The school has protocols and practices in place to ensure that the school's curriculum and accompanying assessments adhere to state and district standards, and it can produce lagging indicators to show the desired effects of these actions.	The school has protocols and practices in place to ensure that the school's curriculum and accompanying assessments adhere to state and district standards.	The school is in the beginning, yet incomplete, stages of drafting protocols and practices to ensure that the school's curriculum and accompanying assessments adhere to state and district standards.	The school has not attempted to ensure that the school's curriculum and accompanying assessments adhere to state and district standards.

Figure 4.1: Scale for leading indicator 3.1—The school curriculum and accompanying assessments adhere to state and district standards.

As leaders move through this scale, they need to help staff face the challenge of digging deeply into state and district standards, establishing common understandings regarding what they ask students to know and be able to do, and ensuring the teaching and assessing in classrooms align to those common understandings. When schools leave staff to interpret standards on their own in isolation, they will most likely interpret them differently. This leads to different learning experiences and expectations for students, which, in turn, can result in staff-created student learning gaps.

Another challenge comes from not having enough high-quality assessments aligned to standards. In many cases, creating these assessments is one of the biggest developmental tasks at this level. The best approach to addressing this challenge is to add assessments incrementally. If teachers gradually but consistently develop assessments over time, a large array of assessments will emerge.

Leading Indicator 3.2

The school curriculum is focused enough that teachers can adequately address it in the time they have available.

This leading indicator focuses on establishing a viable curriculum. This often gets overlooked in the curriculum process; however, schools must truly *teach* content, rather than just *cover* content. In the book *What Works in Schools*, Marzano (2003) identifies a *viable curriculum* as one that teachers can teach in the time available for them to do so. And therein lies the problem. Basic school-calendar mathematics, comparing the number of student contact days and the number of standards, shows the curriculum trap schools must navigate. Generally speaking, a typical school year has about 175 student contact days. However, that number is misleading in regard to the actual days a teacher has to teach the curriculum. The following example represents the reality in most schools.

Beginning with 175 student contact days, we can subtract the first and last day of each semester, as those are commonly logistics and organizational days and involve very little teaching and learning. We must also subtract the days of instruction lost for state and national testing. According to a July 25, 2013, article in *The Washington Post*, one midwestern school district lost as many as nineteen days of instruction, and another lost a month and a half of instruction (Strauss, 2013). If we subtract the lesser number of nineteen days, we have at best 152 student contact days devoted to teaching and learning. This also assumes other days are not lost for unforeseen reasons, such as weather or facility issues.

The number of standards teachers must address and the loss of multiple instructional days have created a nearly impossible teaching and learning situation. To mitigate this issue, district and school leaders should engage teachers in identifying priority standards within each content area and grade level. Tammy Heflebower, Jan K. Hoegh, and Phil Warrick (2014) explain the concept of prioritized standards:

> Prioritized standards are those that have been identified as most essential to a particular grade level, content area, or course. Although it is still important to teach standards that are not deemed prioritized, teachers devote significant time and resources to ensuring that prioritized standards are mastered. (p. 16)

Standards prioritization may occur at the district level, but if it doesn't, it should occur as part of the collaborative team's PLC process answering of critical question 1: What is it we want students to know and be able to do? Marzano et al. (2016) state:

> A collaborative team might do this by looking at each standard for their grade level and content area, having each teacher choose the standards (or parts of standards) he or she thinks are essential, and then discussing and coming to a consensus as to which content is essential. (p. 34)

Heflebower, Hoegh, and Warrick (2014) identify four steps a collaborative team can follow for this process: (1) analyze the standards to become familiar with the material, (2) individually rate the priority of each standard, (3) group the high-priority standards into topics, and (4) review the grouped standards and adjust as necessary.

The key for school leaders is to provide the direction, time, and opportunity for this to happen. Heflebower et al. (2014) recommend that school leaders commit a full day to this process to ensure teams have a clear and common understanding of the priority standards they will teach. Teachers or teacher teams will find it very useful to have a set of criteria they can use to score each standard in this process. For example, the following five criteria help in identifying priority standards. Larry Ainsworth (2003) identifies the first three, and Heflebower, Hoegh, and Warrick (2014) recommend the last two.

1. **Endurance:** The standard has knowledge and skills that will last beyond a class period or single course.
2. **Leverage:** The standard has knowledge and skills that cross over into many domains of learning.
3. **Readiness:** The standard has knowledge and skills important to subsequent content or courses.
4. **Teacher judgment:** Teachers are knowledgeable in the content area and are able to identify more and less important content.
5. **Assessment:** Students have opportunities to learn content that will be assessed.

Using the five criteria, teachers or collaborative teams employ a scoring matrix, like the one in figure 4.2 (page 114), to work through each standard. Each standard scores a point for each criterion it meets. At the end of the scoring process, teachers identify which standards scored highest and which scored lowest. This process makes it much clearer which standards they should prioritize.

One leadership behavior critical to level 3 is to continually monitor the viability of the curriculum. Once teachers establish an initial set of priority standards, school leaders should engage teachers in a reflective process to ensure the standards identified do, in fact, establish a viable curriculum. This process should naturally become a team curriculum review that occurs throughout the year and connects directly to collaborative teams' work as part of the PLC process. Teams can approach this efficiently and effectively by monitoring the number of days they dedicate to instruction for specific standards and making brief reflective notes about the time they allocate to the standards. At the end of the school year, teams should have the opportunity to engage in a reflective exercise and make adjustments to the prioritized standards as necessary prior to the start of the next school year.

Standard	Endurance	Leverage	Readiness	Teacher Judgment	Assessment
CCSS.ELA-Literacy. RI.4.7: Interpret information presented visually, orally, or quantitatively (e.g., in charts, graphs, diagrams, time lines, animations, or interactive elements on web pages) and explain how the information contributes to an understanding of the text in which it appears.	1	1	1	1	1
CCSS.ELA-Literacy. SL.4.5: Add audio recordings and visual displays to presentations when appropriate to enhance the development of main ideas or themes.	1	1	0	0	0

Source for standards: National Governors Association Center for Best Practices (NGA) & Council of Chief State School Officers (CCSSO), 2010.

Figure 4.2: Prioritized standards scoring matrix.

Lagging Indicators

A school can identify and monitor a lagging indicator for leading indicator 3.2 by setting a lagging indicator criterion score of 4.0 out of 5.0 on a Likert scale for staff responses to the following statement: I have the time necessary to teach the priority standards during the school day and school year. The range of scores for this scale is as follows: 1—strongly disagree; 2—disagree; 3—neither disagree nor agree; 4—agree; 5—strongly agree. Leaders ask staff to respond to the statement one time per year. If scores fall below an average of 4.0, then teachers must trim the priority standards.

Other lagging indicators that address leading indicator 3.2 include:

- A document indicating priority standards or topics for each course and grade level is in place.
- A curriculum audit delineates how much time it would take to adequately address the priority standards or topics in each grade level and course.
- Curriculum-team meeting minutes and agendas indicate the viability of priority content or topics and the timing of delivery.

Quick Data and Continuous Improvement

To collect and analyze quick data for this indicator, a school could, for example, have the school's guiding coalition ask three teachers whether they have the time they need to teach, assess, and reteach the priority standards. The coalition then compiles and reviews the results. This provides enough information to determine whether the school is on track, and it does not require as many resources as it does to conduct a survey of all teachers.

Other examples of quick data include the following.

- When asked, teachers can identify the priority standards or topics they teach within a specific curriculum.
- Collaborative teacher teams indicate they have adequate time to reteach and reassess students on priority standards or topics as necessary.
- When surveyed, teachers indicate curriculum maps or pacing guides allow them enough time to adequately address the curriculum.

Leader Accountability

Leader accountability for this indicator involves monitoring whether programs and practices are in place that lead to the curriculum for all content areas being focused enough that it can be addressed in the time available to teachers and that these programs and practices are having their desired effects. Leaders can evaluate their effectiveness using the proficiency scale in figure 4.3 (page 116).

Challenges leaders face as they move through the levels of this scale include the fact that staff who have operated from a coverage mentality have difficulty transitioning to a student-proficiency mentality. This shift might call for a great many in-depth discussions with teachers.

Disagreement regarding what content to address with students may also pose a challenge. We have found that yearly content reviews that provide opportunities for teachers to make changes can effectively address this potential problem.

Sustaining	Applying	Developing	Beginning	Not Attempting
The school continually cultivates information through quick data sources to monitor whether the curriculum for all content areas is focused enough that teachers can adequately address it in the time available, and it takes proper actions to intervene when quick data indicate a potential problem.	The school has protocols and practices in place to ensure that the curriculum for all content areas is focused enough that teachers can adequately address it in the time available, and it can produce lagging indicators to show the desired effects of these actions.	The school has protocols and practices in place to ensure that the curriculum for all content areas is focused enough that teachers can adequately address it in the time available.	The school is in the beginning, yet incomplete, stages of drafting protocols and practices to ensure that the curriculum for all content areas is focused enough that teachers can adequately address it in the time available.	The school has not attempted to ensure that the curriculum for all content areas is focused enough that teachers can adequately address it in the time available.

Figure 4.3: Scale for leading indicator 3.2—The school curriculum is focused enough that teachers can adequately address it in the time they have available.

Finally, leaders might face a challenge if teachers choose content that is not rigorous. Often, teachers seem to choose priority standards based on how easily they can assess them, rather than based on the criteria of endurance, leverage, readiness, teacher judgment, and assessment.

Leading Indicator 3.3

All students have the opportunity to learn the critical content of the curriculum.

A *guaranteed curriculum* means all teachers teach the same content for the same course or grade level. With a guaranteed curriculum, a student in one second-grade class is taught the same content as a student in a different second-grade class, or a student in one ninth-grade English class is taught the same content as a student in a different ninth-grade English class. If the PLC process ensures that a school adequately addresses leading indicator 3.2, then school leaders can attend to this indicator in a straightforward manner. Specifically, if teachers have rigorously identified prioritized standards, then school leaders must ensure that every teacher places equal emphasis on them. School leaders can do so by examining lesson plans. Common assessments designed by collaborative teams are also a good way to determine if the content of the priority standards is receiving equal attention. In schools or courses in which a single teacher teaches the content, ensuring that all students have equal access to priority standards occurs naturally.

School leaders should consider two additional aspects in ensuring a guaranteed curriculum: (1) establishing a comprehensive vocabulary program and (2) providing direct instruction in knowledge application and metacognitive skills.

1. **Establishing a comprehensive vocabulary program:** Robert Marzano, Phil Warrick, and Julia A. Simms (2014) emphasize the importance of vocabulary when they state, "Vocabulary knowledge is so foundational to content knowledge that it should be a focal point of the curriculum" (p. 70). One strategy schools can use to begin developing a comprehensive vocabulary program is to have each teacher or collaborative team identify a set of *guaranteed terms* within a grade level or course's priority content standards. The initial lists developed for a grade level or course could contain forty to sixty terms. As the second step in this strategy, grade-level teachers should meet in vertical teams to reconcile the terms that they should guarantee at each level and in each content area. Ultimately, teams identify approximately twenty to thirty terms per grade level that they guarantee will be taught to all students. Through this process, each teacher or team will have a unique set of guaranteed terms that students will learn, thus helping students establish necessary background knowledge as they progress vertically within each content area.

2. **Providing direct instruction in knowledge application and metacognitive skills:** In the 21st century, schools must address college and career readiness and teach a set of skills that equip students for these two future pursuits. Robert Marzano, Jennifer S. Norford, Michelle Finn, and Douglas Finn III (2017) identify two categories of skills that school must address: (1) cognitive skills and (2) metacognitive skills. Table 4.1 lists common cognitive skills.

Table 4.1: Cognitive Skills

Cognitive Skill	Definition
Generating conclusions	Combining information to create new ideas
Identifying common logical errors	Analyzing conclusions or arguments for validity or truth
Presenting and supporting claims	Using reasons and evidence to support new ideas

continued →

Cognitive Skill	Definition
Navigating digital sources	Finding relevant information online or in electronic resources and assessing its credibility
Using problem solving	Navigating obstacles and limiting conditions to achieve a goal
Using decision making	Selecting the best option from among several good alternatives
Experimenting	Generating explanations for events or phenomena and testing the accuracy of those explanations
Investigating	Identifying questions about a topic, event, or idea and discovering answers, solutions, or predictions
Identifying basic relationships between ideas	Understanding and recognizing how two ideas are connected by time, cause, addition, or contrast
Generating and manipulating mental images	Creating images, symbols, or imagined situations in one's mind and using them to test ideas and solutions

Source: Marzano, Norford, Finn, & Finn, 2017, p. 19.

These cognitive skills have a rich history. Specifically, many of these skills were popular targets of instruction during the 1980s, when a great deal of interest surrounded teaching thinking skills (Marzano et al., 1988). During this period, metacognitive skills also became a focus of instruction. Table 4.2 lists common metacognitive skills.

Table 4.2: Metacognitive Skills

Metacognitive Skill	Definition
Planning for goals and making adjustments	Setting long- or short-term goals, making plans to accomplish those goals, and making adjustments to plans as needed
Staying focused when answers and solutions are not immediately apparent	When engaged in trying to solve a complex problem, recognizing frustration and re-engaging in the task
Pushing the limits of one's knowledge and skills	Setting or adjusting goals so that they require acquiring new knowledge or skills, rather than staying within one's comfort zone
Generating and pursuing one's own standards of excellence	When working toward creating a product, determining what the end result should look like and how success will be judged
Seeking incremental steps	Acquiring knowledge or skills in manageable chunks to avoid becoming overwhelmed, and examining each part's relationship to the whole
Seeking accuracy	Analyzing sources of information for reliability and verifying information by consulting multiple sources

Metacognitive Skill	Definition
Seeking clarity	When taking in new information, noticing one's own confusion and seeking to alleviate it
Resisting impulsivity	Noticing the desire to react or form a conclusion and pausing to revise that response or collect more information
Seeking cohesion and coherence	Monitoring the relationships between individual parts of a system and the relationships between the parts and the whole and making adjustments if they are unstable or not producing the desired results

Source: Marzano, Norford, et al., 2017, p. 22.

As their name implies, metacognitive skills have a strong element of self-analysis, meaning students must think about their own cognitive processes to execute metacognitive skills.

A key aspect of leadership relative to cognitive and metacognitive skills is to help identify which of these skills naturally fall into the existing curriculum and instructional pursuits of different content areas. This allows teachers schoolwide to address one or two of these skills in their work and not have any one group feel responsible for addressing all these skills. Essentially, school leaders must effectively spread out these skills across all curricular areas to share the responsibility schoolwide.

To begin this process, school leaders can have teachers or collaborative teams identify the cognitive and metacognitive skills that have the most natural and direct connections to their content area and curricular standards. Next, a team of lead teachers and administrators can identify which skills to address in each curricular area. This team may choose to have some skills addressed in multiple curricular areas, which is certainly a reasonable decision. However, the very nature of these skills makes them viable across many different disciplines, and some disciplines lend themselves naturally to certain skills. For example, physical education could easily address the metacognitive skill of pushing the limits of one's knowledge, and these teachers could address this skill in nearly every unit they teach. School leaders should make it clear that by identifying the content areas in which teachers will address specific skills, they are by no means precluding teachers from addressing any of these skills when they see a natural connection and a skill fits easily into the work they already do.

Lagging Indicators

A school can identify and monitor a lagging indicator for leading indicator 3.3 by setting the goal to have 100 percent of the collaborative team members submit their priority standards list, vocabulary list, and cognitive and metacognitive skills list to the guiding coalition. The school can then publish the lists on the school or district website for every course or grade level. This level of transparency helps ensure that all students, all staff, and all the community have a keen awareness of the learning expectations for each course and grade level.

Other lagging indicators that address leading indicator 3.3 include:

- Lesson-plan audits indicate teachers address the priority standards or topics within the curriculum.

- Curriculum progress reviews indicate that all teachers teaching specific content or a specific course address the priority standards identified for that content.

- All teachers teaching the same grade level or course use common assessments for priority standards or topics.

Quick Data and Continuous Improvement

To collect and analyze quick data for this indicator, a school could, for example, have teams periodically submit the priority standards they are working on with students and the percentage of their class that has reached proficiency on those priority standards.

Other examples of quick data include the following.

- When asked, teachers can identify the priority standards or topics they currently teach within the curriculum.

- Observations of collaborative teacher-team meetings indicate all the teachers address the priority standards or topics at the same time.

- Special education documents indicate students have the opportunity to learn the curriculum's critical content in accordance with their individualized education plan.

Leader Accountability

Leader accountability for this indicator involves monitoring whether programs and practices are in place that lead to all courses and classes directly addressing the priority standards or topics in the school's curriculum and making sure all students have access to critical content and that these programs and practices have their desired effects. Leaders can evaluate their effectiveness using the proficiency scale in figure 4.4.

Sustaining	Applying	Developing	Beginning	Not Attempting
The school continually cultivates information through quick data sources to monitor that all courses and classes directly address the priority standards or topics in the school's curriculum, making sure all students have access to critical content, and it takes proper actions to intervene when quick data indicate a potential problem.	The school has protocols and practices in place to ensure that all courses and classes directly address the priority standards or topics in the school's curriculum, making sure all students have access to critical content, and it can produce lagging indicators to show the desired effects of these actions.	The school has protocols and practices in place to ensure that all courses and classes directly address the priority standards or topics in the school's curriculum, making sure all students have access to critical content.	The school is in the beginning, yet incomplete, stages of drafting protocols and practices to ensure that all courses and classes directly address the priority standards or topics in the school's curriculum, making sure all students have access to critical content.	The school has not attempted to ensure that all courses and classes directly address the priority standards or topics in the school's curriculum, making sure all students have access to critical content.

Figure 4.4: Scale for leading indicator 3.3—All students have the opportunity to learn the critical content of the curriculum.

As leaders move through this scale, they will face a challenge if the same course has different outcome expectations based on how the course groups students (often seen as advanced courses versus regular courses, where the same course outcomes should be expected). For example, the school might break down algebra into sections of advanced algebra, regular algebra, and remedial algebra.

Another challenge occurs when a school does not have processes in place to ensure that teachers reach consensus regarding priority standards for each course. Leaders commonly do not monitor the intended, implemented, and attained curricula, which causes problems.

Leading Indicator 3.4

The school establishes clear and measurable goals that are focused on critical needs regarding improving overall student achievement at the school level.

This leading indicator focuses on the development of schoolwide student achievement goals. When schools attend to this leading indicator well, it provides a clear vision for student achievement goals across academic departments, collaborative teams, and individual teachers so they can work on these goals in a well-coordinated joint effort.

One of the best ways to write schoolwide goals is in the SMART goal format (strategic, measurable, attainable, results oriented, time bound) (Conzemius & O'Neill, 2014). School improvement goals should express a percentage of students who will score at a proficient level or higher on state assessments and district benchmark assessments. These goals should address achievement for the student body as a whole and efforts to close achievement gaps between student populations of different ethnicities and socioeconomic levels.

The following examples show schoolwide goals written as SMART goals and how collaborative teams can write goals to work in conjunction with the schoolwide goals. Hence, each collaborative team focuses on its specific group of students, and by doing this, the teams collectively address the schoolwide goals.

School goals

- At least 75 percent of students will score at a proficient level or higher in mathematics, as measured by district benchmark assessments and state assessments.

- At least 65 percent of economically disadvantaged students will score at a proficient level or higher in mathematics, as measured by district benchmark assessments and state assessments.

Algebra team goals

- At least 75 percent of algebra students will score at a proficient level or higher, as measured by district benchmark assessments and state assessments.

- At least 65 percent of economically disadvantaged algebra students will score at a proficient level or higher, as measured by district benchmark assessments and state assessments.

To continue with this example, assume each collaborative team for a specific course or level of mathematics develops similar goals for its team. Collectively, the teams all work toward the schoolwide goal, yet individually, they direct their focus to students in their courses at that time. When schoolwide goals and collaborative team goals reach alignment, collaborative teams can analyze the common assessments they give based on the percentages identified in the teams' student achievement goals. This allows team members to continually monitor student progress toward the end goal and to enact timely interventions if students are underperforming and not moving toward the proficiency levels established in the school and team goals. Leading indicator 3.5 (page 124) addresses developing systems and protocols for that process.

Lagging Indicators

A school can identify and monitor a lagging indicator for leading indicator 3.4 by setting and posting schoolwide goals and having teams set SMART goals for each priority standard for each course. Teams then share their goals with the entire staff and monitor progress throughout the year. Teams can compare results from year to year and make adjustments based on the previous year's performance; and the cycle continues.

Other lagging indicators that address leading indicator 3.4 include:

- The school and individual teams establish written goals as a percentage of students who will score at a proficient level or higher on benchmark assessments or state assessments.

- The school and individual teams establish written goals for eliminating differences in achievement for students of different socioeconomic levels or differing ethnicities.

- Written goals contain specific timelines for each goal, including individuals or teams responsible for the goal.

Quick Data and Continuous Improvement

To collect and analyze quick data for this indicator, a school could, for example, have the school leadership team gather progress updates toward teacher-team goals each quarter. Teams then reflect on and share whether they are on track to meet their goals by the end of the year.

Other examples of quick data include the following.

- When asked, teachers can describe their school's progress toward its schoolwide goals.

- When asked, teachers can describe specific schoolwide achievement goals that relate directly to content they have responsibility for teaching.

Leader Accountability

Leader accountability for this indicator involves monitoring whether programs and practices are in place that lead to clear and measurable goals with specific timelines focused on critical needs regarding improving student achievement at the school level and that these programs and practices are having their desired effects. Leaders can evaluate their effectiveness using the proficiency scale in figure 4.5.

Sustaining	Applying	Developing	Beginning	Not Attempting
The school continually cultivates information through quick data sources to monitor a schoolwide focus on and progress toward the established goals, and it takes proper actions to intervene when quick data indicate a potential problem.	The school has established clear and measurable goals with specific timelines focused on critical needs regarding improving student achievement at the school level, and it can produce lagging indicators to show the desired effects of these actions.	The school has established clear and measurable goals with specific timelines focused on critical needs regarding improving student achievement at the school level.	The school is in the beginning, yet incomplete, stages of establishing clear and measurable goals with specific timelines focused on critical needs regarding improving student achievement at the school level.	The school has not attempted to establish clear and measurable goals with specific timelines focused on critical needs regarding improving student achievement at the school level.

Figure 4.5: Scale for leading indicator 3.4—The school establishes clear and measurable goals that are focused on critical needs regarding improving overall student achievement at the school level.

Challenges leaders face as they move through the levels of this scale include the fact that a lack of prior data makes setting proficiency goals for priority standards difficult (for example, determining a goal's attainability is hard without knowing how students have done on the standard in the past).

Staff might also find this challenging because they are not accustomed to setting goals for internal assessment results. Finally, while goals might exist on paper, leaders will find it challenging to reach the goals if the school's culture does not support the pursuit of achieving the goals.

Leading Indicator 3.5

The school analyzes, interprets, and uses data to regularly monitor progress toward school achievement goals.

This leading indicator requires a comprehensive system of assessment to analyze, interpret, and use data to monitor progress toward student achievement goals. Marzano (2018) recommends employing three systems of assessment, as depicted in figure 4.6: (1) classroom assessments, (2) interim assessments, and (3) year-end assessments.

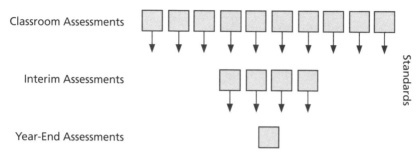

Source: Marzano, 2018, p. 6.

Figure 4.6: Three systems of assessment.

Figure 4.6 indicates that the three levels of assessments have very different frequencies of use. Clearly, classroom assessments most closely resemble students' day-to-day life, and students most frequently experience this type of assessment. Unfortunately, measurement experts have criticized classroom assessments as having a number of weaknesses, such as the following.

- Teachers who prepare them have little or no preparation for such tasks.
- Teachers score the assessments using idiosyncratic and erratic methods.
- Teachers base the assessments on erroneous beliefs about assessment.
- Teachers do not use a wide variety of assessment practices.
- Teachers prepare the assessments too quickly and without sufficient vetting.
- The assessments result in imprecise evaluative judgments from teachers.

These weaknesses notwithstanding, Marzano (2018) has shown how teachers can design and implement a system of classroom assessments that renders the assessments as reliable and valid as year-end and interim assessments. Additionally, he details a process that school leaders can use to measure student growth on specific topics using classroom assessments. He says leaders should ensure that multiple parallel assessments are designed for each priority standard or topic in the guaranteed and viable curriculum (Marzano, 2018). For each topic, teachers administer common pretests and post-tests. That way, teachers can measure student growth on each priority topic. With such a system in place, school leaders can set and monitor SMART goals at the standard or topic level.

Next are interim assessments. M. Christina Schneider, Karla Egan, and Marc Julian (2013) define them in the following way: "Interim assessments (sometimes referred to as benchmark assessments) are standardized, periodic assessments of students throughout a school year or subject course" (p. 58). Teachers can also use these to set student achievement goals and monitor progress toward those goals. The obvious problem with using year-end and interim assessments exclusively is that this ignores the most frequent type of assessment.

Finally, year-end assessments are certainly an important source of information with which to monitor student achievement. Schneider and colleagues (2013) describe them as follows:

> States administer year-end assessments to gauge how well schools and districts are performing with respect to the state standards. These tests are broad in scope because test content is cumulative and sampled across the state-level content standards to support inferences regarding how much a student can do in relation to all of the state standards. Simply stated, these are summative tests. The term *year-end assessment* can be a misnomer because these assessments are sometimes administered toward the end of a school year, usually in March or April and sometimes during the first semester of the school year. (p. 59)

Lagging Indicators

A school can identify and monitor a lagging indicator for leading indicator 3.5 by ensuring that 100 percent of teams establish and utilize common assessments for every priority standard. In addition, all teams must report the number of students who reach proficiency on every priority standard after they administer and score common assessments.

Other lagging indicators that address leading indicator 3.5 include:

- School leaders make available reports, graphs, and charts on overall progress toward student achievement goals.
- Collaborative teams update data walls to show progress toward student achievement goals.
- Teachers regularly use and report results for multiple types of assessments (for example, benchmark and common assessments) to monitor progress toward student achievement goals.

Quick Data and Continuous Improvement

To collect and analyze quick data for this indicator, a school could, for example, have the guiding coalition pull the priority standard data and review the progress teams make on a quarterly basis. If teams have data missing, the school leader provides guidance and support to ensure such data are readily available in the future.

Other examples of quick data include the following.

- When asked, faculty and staff can describe the different types of reports available to them.
- Collaborative teams provide data briefings at faculty meetings regarding progress toward student achievement goals.
- Students track their own progress toward achievement goals.

Leader Accountability

Leader accountability for this indicator involves monitoring whether programs and practices are in place that lead to monitoring progress toward school achievement goals and that these programs and practices are achieving their desired effects. Leaders can evaluate their effectiveness using the proficiency scale in figure 4.7.

Sustaining	Applying	Developing	Beginning	Not Attempting
The school continually cultivates information through quick data sources to ensure data are used regularly to monitor progress toward school achievement goals, and it takes proper actions to intervene when quick data indicate a potential problem.	The school has established systems and practices for monitoring progress toward school achievement goals, and it can produce lagging indicators to show the desired effects of these actions.	The school has established systems and practices for monitoring progress toward school achievement goals.	The school is in the beginning, yet incomplete, stages of establishing systems and practices for monitoring progress toward school achievement goals.	The school has not attempted to establish systems and practices for monitoring progress toward school achievement goals.

Figure 4.7: Scale for leading indicator 3.5—The school analyzes, interprets, and uses data to regularly monitor progress toward school achievement goals.

Challenges leaders face as they move through the levels of this scale include the fact that monitoring progress on every priority standard can challenge a school when it first gets started. We recommend teams begin by monitoring progress on three to four priority standards they think are most important.

Teams also commonly feel challenged because they gather data, but they never do anything with them. Also, they might lack awareness of how much incremental progress they have to make to reach the student achievement goals (they set no benchmarks along the way, only year-end goals).

Leading Indicator 3.6

The school establishes appropriate school- and classroom-level programs and practices to help students meet individual achievement goals when data indicate interventions are needed.

This leading indicator focuses on helping students learn and grow by implementing collective intervention and extension practices operating as flexible systems that respond fluidly to meet students' needs. The task for school leadership is to identify, implement, and monitor these systems. As Richard DuFour, Rebecca DuFour, Robert Eaker, and Gayle Karhanek (2004) state, "Any system of interventions for students will only be as effective as the process that is in place both to monitor student learning and to respond when students experience difficulty" (p. 60).

Implementation of response to intervention (RTI) strategies during the 2010s has seen positive and productive developments as school leaders have begun to change paradigms and see the concept of RTI occur in a number of different ways. For example, school leaders have recognized that they must also provide extensions to students to go above and beyond what is taught as part of RTI practices. To successfully implement this leading indicator, school leaders need to think about both classroom and schoolwide practices that support student learning and how the two can work in harmony to serve all students. School leaders should consider several guiding questions.

- Does our current use of time provide for appropriate learning interventions?
- Do our staff have the knowledge and skills necessary to enact effective interventions?
- How will we monitor our interventions to make sure they work?

This leading indicator connects directly to leading indicator 1.4 and the PLC process a school puts in place. In fact, through the use of the PLC process, collaborative teams initiate successful intervention strategies with a high level of efficiency. For this to occur, each teacher on a collaborative team needs to realize that collectively they can much more efficiently and effectively help all students learn.

To help develop collective ownership of student achievement, school leaders should openly encourage and expect the use of strategies such as flexible student grouping based on learner needs. Creating time and space for these types of interventions is a direct function of school leadership and often involves specifying intervention time within the schedule for collaborative teams to group and regroup students based on their needs. Additionally, the use of flexible grouping allows at least one teacher group to address students who are ready for learning extensions. Teachers can find this strategy effective in both elementary and secondary schools.

Figure 4.8 shows an elementary example of intervention time from Epperly Heights Elementary in the Mid-Del School District in Oklahoma. The school calls its intervention time *mustang stampede* time. During this time, all teachers work with students in the area of reading interventions Tuesday through Thursday each week. The different colors in figure 4.8 represent different schedules students are on. The important part of this figure is that no matter what schedule a student is on (red, yellow, blue, or green), he or she participates in mustang stampede every day from 9:10 a.m. to 9:40 a.m.

	Red	**Yellow**	**Blue**	**Green**
9:10–9:40 a.m.	Schoolwide Mustang Stampede Tuesday, Wednesday, and Thursday			
9:45–10:25 a.m.	Parker/Whiting Third	McCollum/ Whiting Third	Boeckman/ Whiting Third	Clayton/Whiting Third
10:25–11:05 a.m.	Musselman Fourth	Perry Fourth	Klick Fourth	Piersall Fourth
11:05–11:45 a.m.	Bennett Fifth	Rodney Fifth	Woodard Fifth	Cox Fifth
12:35–1:15 p.m.	PreK	PreK	PreK	PreK
1:20–2:00 p.m.	Harris Kindergarten	Tolman Kindergarten	Fleshman Kindergarten	White Kindergarten
2:05–2:45 p.m.	Branton First	Shaw First	Stults First	Matthews First
2:50–3:30 p.m.	C. Phillips Second	Stoddard Second	Stringfellow Second	Brathwaite Second

Source: © 2015 by Epperly Heights Elementary.

Figure 4.8: Epperly Heights Elementary mustang stampede intervention schedule.

Figure 4.9 (page 130) shows a middle school intervention schedule from South Sioux City Middle School in South Sioux City, Nebraska. The *what I need* (WIN) intervention time occurs Tuesday through Friday schoolwide. Just as the name indicates, this time is designed for students to receive academic interventions or extensions for their learning. These interventions and extentions fit students' specific

---

Tuesday Through Friday Schedule

First period: 8:10–8:53 a.m.
Second period: 8:57–9:40 a.m.
Third period: 9:44–10:27 a.m.
Fourth period: 10:31–11:14 a.m.
Fifth and sixth period: 11:18 a.m.–1:19 p.m.

Lunch Groups

Group 1: 11:15–11:50 a.m.   **Group 4:** 11:30 a.m.–12:05 p.m. **Group 7:** 11:50 a.m.–12:25 p.m.
Group 2: 11:20–11:55 a.m.   **Group 5:** 11:35 a.m.–12:10 p.m. **Group 8:** 11:55 a.m.–12:30 p.m.
Group 3: 11:25 a.m.–12:00 p.m. **Group 6:** 11:40 a.m.–12:15 p.m. **Group 9:** 12:00–12:35 p.m.

Seventh period: 1:23–1:51 p.m. (WIN time)
Eighth period: 1:55–2:38 p.m.
Ninth period: 2:42–3:25 p.m.

Source: © 2017 by South Sioux City Middle School.

Figure 4.9: South Sioux City Middle School WIN schedule.

needs as learners based on assessments measuring the priority standards teachers identified for each content at each grade level.

Figure 4.10 shows the *working on work* (WOW) intervention schedule from Round Rock High School in Round Rock, Texas. During WOW time, all teachers are available in their classrooms for students to seek help in any content area. To access a teacher for tutoring, retesting, or any type of general academic help, a student obtains a WOW pass to see a specific teacher during WOW time. Because seniors are allowed to have an open, off-campus period each day, WOW time is purposely placed between the third and fourth periods to allow some students to leave campus as usual unless they need to seek help during WOW time.

Period 1 and period 5: 9:05–10:25 a.m.
Period 2 and period 6: 10:31–11:51 a.m.
Period 3 and period 7
  • **First lunch:** 11:57 a.m.–12:27 p.m.
  • **Second lunch:** 12:38–1:14 p.m.
  • **Third lunch:** 1:25–2:02 p.m.
WOW period: 2:07–2:42 p.m.
Period 4 and period 8: 2:48–4:08 p.m.

Source: © 2011 by Round Rock High School.

Figure 4.10: Round Rock High School WOW schedule.

Another highly effective use of time as a learning intervention is to build an intervention class into the master schedule staffed by a teacher who has expert knowledge in a specific content area. School leaders must plan for this in the scheduling process, and they should make it their ultimate goal to have a content-area expert in the intervention class each period of the day, if possible. We know a large suburban high school that makes a mathematics intervention classroom available to any mathematics student who has fallen behind or who simply wants to make time for additional help on concepts he or she struggles with. At any one time, students from four to five different levels of mathematics may come into the room to get help or engage in a learning opportunity with the scheduled mathematics teacher. A teacher can send students to the mathematics intervention room from his or her mathematics class if he or she feels they would benefit from it, or those students can obtain a pass and go in on their own during study hall.

School leaders should also consider how they can equip staff with resources of specific intervention strategies that will help them address students' learning needs. At Grove Valley Elementary School in the Deer Creek School District in Oklahoma, a team of school leaders created an ebook manual of reading intervention strategies for classroom teachers (D. Jones, personal communication, May 9, 2017). The ebook offers teachers a choice of strategies matched to specific reading skills and clearly explains how to implement them. It also includes video examples of how to execute the interventions.

Monitoring systems also carry importance for this leading indicator. Such systems should work in conjunction with the school's PLC process. For example, collaborative teams schoolwide should use assessment data from their work to inform the need for interventions and make decisions about which specific intervention strategies to use for individual students. In this way, the school's intervention times and resources are directly connected to the needs collaborative teams are monitoring in their students. Thus the systems are interdependent within the school as a PLC. These systems can be technology based or involve the use of a physical data wall or data board. School leaders should consider two key conditions for any monitoring system. First, collaborative teams must regularly update and review the data in the system. Second, the system must monitor all students' progress or lack of progress. A monitoring system that includes these two conditions can better inform the need for interventions. Figure 4.11 (page 132) shows a data wall system that Grove Valley Elementary uses to monitor student progress.

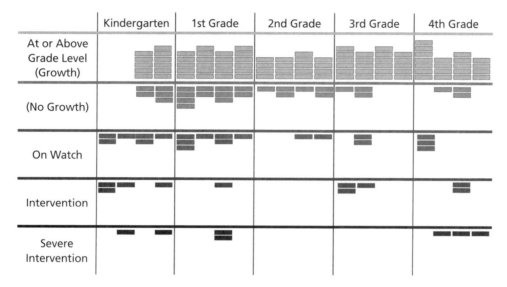

Figure 4.11: Grove Valley Elementary data wall.

The Grove Valley Elementary data wall resides in the school conference room and is covered by doors when the conference room is in use. The data wall contains multiple levels for monitoring student progress throughout the year. Student names appear on colored magnets that correlate to the students' initially assessed level (red = severe intervention, yellow = intervention, blue = on watch, green = at or above grade level) in reading and also in mathematics. As teachers give common assessments throughout the year, grade-level teams analyze the data and move students up or down through the different levels and make intervention and extension plans accordingly. The school includes one additional category, not shown in figure 4.11, that indicates students who perform on grade level but show no growth during the year. Students in this level of learning can benefit from classroom-level intervention strategies to ensure they don't begin to slide backward.

Lagging Indicators

A school can identify and monitor a lagging indicator for leading indicator 3.6 by establishing a goal that 100 percent of students will have the opportunity for extra time, extra help, and, when ready, extensions for every priority standard. Throughout the year, the school expects teacher teams to group and regroup students based on their needs for each priority standard. The school builds the master schedule to include time for every grade level to provide interventions and extensions. Teams keep track of student groupings and monitor achievement progress.

Other lagging indicators that address leading indicator 3.6 include:

- The school designs its schedule so students can engage in intervention opportunities during the school day.
- The school has programs in place to extend and enhance individual student academic achievement.
- The school has Extended School Year services in place.

Quick Data and Continuous Improvement

To collect and analyze quick data for this indicator, a school could, for example, choose five students who are struggling with a priority standard and five students who have already achieved proficiency with it. Teachers interview both groups in an attempt to determine which interventions are working for them.

Other examples of quick data include the following.

- When asked, teachers can explain intervention opportunities available for their students.
- Specific data sources indicate which students are currently identified for intervention.
- Collaborative-team meeting minutes indicate ongoing progress monitoring for students receiving specific interventions.

Leader Accountability

Leader accountability for this indicator involves monitoring whether programs and practices are in place that lead to schoolwide and classroom interventions to help students meet individual achievement goals when data indicate interventions are needed and that these programs and practices are having their desired effects. Leaders can evaluate their effectiveness using the proficiency scale in figure 4.12 (page 134).

Many of the challenges leaders face as they move through the levels of this scale center on the changes associated with building a school schedule that allows extra time and support for all students. Alteration in a school schedule can change people's lives, which, in turn, can also upset them. Another challenge is that although a school might have an effective schedule in place, teachers and leaders may not pay enough attention to the quality of instruction occurring within that schedule for it to help students meet individual achievement goals.

Sustaining	Applying	Developing	Beginning	Not Attempting
The school continually cultivates information through quick data sources to monitor that appropriate schoolwide and classroom intervention programs and practices are used to help students meet individual achievement goals, and it takes proper actions to intervene when quick data indicate a potential problem.	The school has protocols and practices in place to ensure that appropriate schoolwide and classroom intervention programs and practices are used to help students meet individual achievement goals when data indicate interventions are needed, and it can produce lagging indicators to show the desired effects of these actions.	The school has protocols and practices in place to ensure that appropriate schoolwide and classroom intervention programs and practices are used to help students meet individual achievement goals when data indicate interventions are needed.	The school is in the beginning, yet incomplete, stages of drafting protocols and practices to ensure that appropriate schoolwide and classroom intervention programs and practices are used to help students meet individual achievement goals when data indicate interventions are needed.	The school has not attempted to ensure that appropriate schoolwide and classroom intervention programs and practices are used to help students meet individual achievement goals when data indicate interventions are needed.

Figure 4.12: Scale for leading indicator 3.6—The school establishes appropriate school- and classroom-level programs and practices to help students meet individual achievement goals when data indicate interventions are needed.

Level 3 Transformations

Level 3 of the HRS model focuses on ensuring a guaranteed and viable curriculum. Actions to this end include the school establishing access to important content for all students and setting and monitoring goals regarding that content. We have seen some powerful results when school leaders take on this perspective. The following are a few examples.

A key aspect of NYOS Charter School's level 3 work has been establishing a comprehensive vocabulary program. Here, Jenna Tintera, assistant principal at NYOS, speaks directly to what this work has done for her school:

> Our implementation of a schoolwide Tier 2 and 3 academic vocabulary program has enabled students and teachers to clearly define the academic content for each unit of study. But the big game changer for us was the implementation of a monitoring system for Tier 1 vocabulary. We have seen dramatic increases in our oral and written English language proficiency as a result of monitoring the growth of our ESL students and planning across the grade level for their Tier 1 vocabulary needs. (J. Tintera, personal communication, August 8, 2017)

In 2016, the Texas Education Agency recognized NYOS as one of the top-performing Title I schools in the state of Texas.

Another key aspect of level 3 of the HRS model is the implementation of coordinated intervention systems. Tom McGuire, principal at South Sioux City Middle School in South Sioux City, Nebraska, has seen the development of his school's intervention system pay off for students schoolwide:

> Our goal at South Sioux City Middle School is for all students to learn at high levels. We believe that through the use of WIN time we are able to meet each student at his or her instructional level with each priority standard. WIN time has empowered our students to be advocates for themselves as individual scholars. Our achievement data continues to have a positive trend line, and WIN time has played a big role with that. In year 3 of using WIN time, six out of nine assessed areas were above the status norm on the MAP (Measures of Academic Progress) assessment. Two years ago, we were well below the status norm in all tested areas. (T. McGuire, personal communication, August 20, 2017)

Principal Trina Lake at Break-O-Day Elementary School in New Whiteland, Indiana, finds that using the HRS model to identify high-leverage standards and vocabulary terms has led to a more solid guaranteed and viable curriculum. The school now has its standards mapped out, and staff know how to better address individual student needs by student and by skill. Regarding the work at level 3, Mrs. Lake says, "We no longer feel confused by the gaps we see in student learning because we know what they are and how to fill them" (T. Lake, personal communication, August 29, 2017).

Conclusion

Leadership for level 3 of the HRS model focuses on creating a guaranteed and viable curriculum. Such an emphasis addresses the first of the six critical questions Rick described in the introductory chapter: What is it we want students to learn? This level has six leading indicators. For a school to declare itself highly reliable relative to level 3, leaders must generate lagging indicators for each leading indicator with clear criteria for success. Even after the school has met these success criteria, the school must continue to collect quick data to monitor and react to variations in its performance on these six indicators.

Chapter 5

Standards-Referenced Reporting

● ● ●

Levels 1–3 of the HRS model are part and parcel of the work in which all schools must engage. In effect, the leading indicators for levels 1, 2, and 3 represent those things every school must continuously attend to if it aspires to function effectively. Levels 4 and 5 of the HRS model represent systems changes. The major change at level 4 has schools shift from a whole-school perspective to an individual student perspective. Whereas certainly some attention to individual students occurs at levels 1, 2, and 3, at level 4, the individual student is the focus of data collection and reporting.

Level 4 of the HRS model directly addresses question 2 of the six critical questions Rick described in the introduction: How will we know if students are learning? It also addresses question 3: How will we respond when students don't learn? As mentioned previously, HRS level 4 answers these questions with a focus on individual students. It does so through standards-referenced reporting.

At the level of standards-referenced reporting, a school attends to and operationalizes what Hattie (2015) identifies as the highest-ranking and third-highest-ranking of the 195 variables related to achievement: teacher estimates of student achievement and student self-reported grades. Both of these require reporting at the individual student level.

Level 4 of the HRS model has two leading indicators.

4.1 The school establishes clear and measurable goals focused on critical needs regarding improving achievement of individual students.

4.2 The school analyzes, interprets, and uses data to regularly monitor progress toward achievement goals for individual students.

Leading Indicator 4.1

The school establishes clear and measurable goals focused on critical needs regarding improving achievement of individual students.

As we have described, at the heart of a standards-referenced system lies a focus on individual students. Also note that at the heart of this indicator, we find student status and growth. *Status* refers to a student's current level of achievement. *Growth* refers to the difference between a student's current status and his or her initial status. Although differentiating between status and growth seems like a simple concept to understand, a school will have difficulty operationalizing it unless it articulates learning goals for students as proficiency scales. Figure 5.1 depicts a sample proficiency scale.

Score 4.0	The student researches a solution that addresses a cause of weathering and erosion (for example, investigate the rate of erosion by a local stream, determine how human activity impacts this rate, and implement a solution that reduces the effect of human activity, such as planting vegetation by the stream bank or maintaining a designated trail through the area).	
	Score 3.5	In addition to score 3.0 performance, the student has partial success at score 4.0 content.
Score 3.0	The student identifies factors that contribute to weathering and erosion (for example, explains how weathering and erosion are caused by water, ice, wind, and vegetation, and identifies factors that increase the effect and rate of weathering and erosion).	
	Score 2.5	The student has no major errors or omissions regarding score 2.0 content, and partial success at score 3.0 content.
Score 2.0	The student recognizes or recalls specific vocabulary (for example, *erosion, sediment, water, weathering,* and *wind*) and performs basic processes such as: • Explain the difference between weathering and erosion (weathering breaks down rocks and minerals into smaller pieces, whereas erosion moves the smaller pieces from place to place) • Identify causes of weathering (for example, precipitation, ice, wind, acid rain, water, and vegetation) • Identify causes of erosion (for example, wind, water, gravity, snow, and ice). • Compare the effects of weathering and erosion over time (for example, a river may not seem to be causing erosion when observed daily but can carve out canyons over long spans of time) • Explain how erosion causes deposition of weathered sediments	
	Score 1.5	The student has partial success at score 2.0 content and major errors or omissions regarding score 3.0 content.
Score 1.0	With help, the student has partial success at score 2.0 content and score 3.0 content.	
	Score 0.5	With help, the student has partial success at score 2.0 content but not at score 3.0 content.
Score 0.0	Even with help, the student has no success.	

Figure 5.1: Scale for a grade 4 unit on weathering and erosion.

A number of resources describe the nature and function of a proficiency scale (Marzano, 2006, 2010, 2018; Marzano et al., 2016; Marzano, Norford, et al., 2017). Briefly, proficiency scales describe expected levels of understanding and skill for specific topics, which we refer to as *measurement topics*. Educators should state curriculum for each subject area and grade level as proficiency scales. We recommend about twelve to thirty-five proficiency scales for each subject area and grade level. Teachers should use these scales to track each student's beginning status and current status. For specific details about how to design and score assessments using this scale, see the references cited at the beginning of this paragraph.

Teachers could report this information in a status report, as depicted in figure 5.2. The dark part of each bar graph in figure 5.2 represents the student's initial status on a particular topic, and the light part of the bar graph represents the student's final status. Thus, the light part shows the student's gain on the proficiency scale represented by the graph. This type of report can and should be an addendum to traditional report cards (see Marzano, 2006, 2010, 2018; Marzano, Norford, et al., 2017). Collaborative teams can also use it as a source of data to monitor the status and growth of their students (see Marzano et al., 2016).

Teachers can combine a student's final scores on each topic using a weighted or unweighted average. This average can then be translated into a traditional overall grade using a conversion scale such as:

- A = 3.00 to 4.00
- B = 2.50 to 2.99
- C = 2.00 to 2.49
- D = 1.00 to 1.99
- F = Below 1.00

The convention of a status report provides a great deal of information to students, teachers, administrators, and parents. School leaders can use this convention to make the process of securing a guaranteed and viable curriculum (level 3 of the HRS model) focused and highly transparent.

Language Arts		
Reading:		
Word Recognition and Vocabulary	2.5	
Reading for Main Idea	1.5	
Literary Analysis	2.0	
Writing:		
Language Conventions	3.5	
Organization and Focus	2.5	
Research and Technology	1.0	

Figure 5.2: Sample student status report.

continued →

Language Arts									
Evaluation and Revision	2.5								
Writing Applications	3.0								
Listening and Speaking:									
Comprehension	3.0								
Organization and Delivery	3.0								
Analysis and Evaluation of Oral Media	2.5								
Speaking Applications	2.5								
Life Skills:									
Participation	4.0								
Work Completion	3.5								
Behavior	3.5								
Working in Groups	3.0								
Average for Language Arts	2.46								

Source: DuFour & Marzano, 2011, p. 136. © 2007 by Marzano & Associates.

Having clear and measurable goals in place for improving individual student achievement allows school leaders to evaluate student progress and celebrate when students achieve their goals. School leaders can best establish such goals when they set them as part of a goal-setting process like that outlined in figure 5.3. Setting goals and forming plans compose part of leading indicator 4.1, whereas monitoring progress and evaluating whether students have achieved success compose part of leading indicator 4.2 (page 145). In the classroom, they are not separated; rather, they flow as one ongoing cycle.

Figure 5.3: Goal-setting process.

It is important that students take part in the goal-setting process. Leaders should clarify the expectations that staff help students set goals, form plans, monitor progress, and evaluate success, but they need to let staff innovate in finding the best ways to do that with individual students. Sometimes, simple solutions work very well. For example, in some classrooms at Break-O-Day Elementary, students simply write their individual goals on sticky notes as they work through the curriculum.

In other classrooms at Break-O-Day Elementary, students use templates to set goals and form plans, like that pictured in figure 5.4. Students begin by logging their pretest scores. Then they set a goal and form an action plan to accomplish the goal. These become part of a data binder or data notebook that students can use to help them set goals throughout the school year.

3.W.1—Writing in Response to Literature and Informational Texts

Level 4	I can go above and beyond what is expected.
Level 3	I can write in response to literature and informational texts. My response completely answers the question and includes two or more details to support my answer. I can write in complete sentences with correct capitalization and punctuation.
Level 2	I can respond to reading when given a graphic organizer.
Level 1	I can do this with help.

My Baseline: 2			My Goal: 3.5		
How's it going?					
				My plan is to pay attention to my friends when we work together and pay closer attention to my teacher.	
4.0	★	★	★		
3.5					
3.0	★	★	★		
2.5					
2.0	★	★	★	★	★	★
1.5					
1.0	★	★	★	★	★	★
0.5					
	Attempt #1 Date: 9/1	Attempt #2 Date: 9/10	Attempt #3 Date: 9/22	Attempt #4 Date: ___	Attempt #5 Date: ___	Attempt #6 Date: ___

Figure 5.4: Goal-setting and planning template.

Regardless of how staff work with students to set goals, they should continually work on shifting ownership from staff to students. The potential power in the system created by having a guaranteed and viable curriculum coupled with proficiency scales lies in students utilizing the system to advance their learning. As Marzano (2017) points out in *The New Art and Science of Teaching*, "Specific mental states and processes in learners' minds are the mediating variable between effective application of instructional strategies and enhanced student learning" (p. 5). It is possible to spend a lot of time, effort, and energy developing proficiency scales and having students set goals and form plans and gain little to no resulting student achievement to show for it. This can occur if students simply go through the motions and comply with teachers' requests, rather than truly have a sense of agency around the work. To avoid this, leaders should look for and cultivate the following student behaviors (adapted from Marzano, 2017).

- Students can explain the proficiency scales related to their learning goals in their own words.
- Students recognize their learning goals and can explain when lessons address them.
- Students can explain how classroom activities relate to their learning goals.
- Students can explain the progression of content on the proficiency scales related to their learning goals.
- Students can explain how they have progressed on the proficiency scales related to their learning goals.
- Students can explain what they need to do to get to the next level of performance on the proficiency scales related to their learning goals.

When school leaders focus their efforts on cultivating these student behaviors, student agency increases. The likelihood of generating student achievement results greatly increases when this occurs.

Lagging Indicators

A school can identify and monitor a lagging indicator for leading indicator 4.1 by establishing that all staff members assist students so 100 percent of the student body set goals and form plans in at least one course or subject. Each staff member shares examples of three students' goals and action plans. This allows staff to see multiple examples of student goals aligned to the proficiency scales. It also allows school leaders to monitor whether the examples meet the lagging indicator for this leading indicator.

Other lagging indicators that address leading indicator 4.1 include:

- Teachers establish written goals for each student in terms of his or her performance on state assessments, benchmark assessments, or common assessments.
- Teachers establish written goals accompanied by proficiency scales for each student in terms of his or her knowledge gain.
- Student-led conferences focus on individual student goals.

Quick Data and Continuous Improvement

To collect and analyze quick data for this indicator, a school could have at least one different staff member go into every classroom once per month and ask students questions about their learning. The staff at Clark-Pleasant Community Schools ask the following questions.

- "What are you currently working on or learning about?"
- "What is your current level on the proficiency scale related to this learning?"
- "What was your level of achievement when you first began this concept or skill?"
- "What is your goal for this concept or skill?"
- "What do you need to learn and be able to do to get to the next level?"
- "How do you celebrate success when you reach a goal? Do your teacher and class celebrate with you?"
- "How does your teacher use class time to help you reach your learning goals?"
- "What have you done in class to help you reach your goals?"

These questions appear in a Google Form, which allows all staff to quickly record responses and monitor their general tone and direction. The scope of these questions serves as a quick check for leading indicator 4.1. The questions also serve as a quick check for leading indicator 4.2. Gathering this type of quick data comes with the advantage that it also can impact the student culture around goal setting. For example, when students see that a vast majority of their peers have identified what they need to do to move to the next level, such behavior becomes an expectation for all students.

Other examples of quick data include the following.

- When asked, students can explain their current status regarding goals specific to them.
- Students keep data notebooks and track their progress on their individual goals.
- When asked, parents express that they have awareness of their children's individual goals.

Leader Accountability

Leader accountability for this indicator involves monitoring whether programs and practices are in place that lead to clear and measurable goals being established that are focused on critical needs regarding improving achievement of individual students and that these programs and practices are having their desired effects. Leaders can evaluate their effectiveness using the proficiency scale in figure 5.5.

Sustaining	Applying	Developing	Beginning	Not Attempting
The school continually cultivates information through quick data sources to monitor that clear and measurable goals are established and focused on critical needs regarding improving achievement of individual students, and it takes proper actions to intervene when quick data indicate a potential problem.	The school has protocols and practices in place to ensure that clear and measurable goals are established and focused on critical needs regarding improving achievement of individual students, and it can produce lagging indicators to show the desired effects of these actions.	The school has protocols and practices in place to ensure that clear and measurable goals are established and focused on critical needs regarding improving achievement of individual students.	The school is in the beginning, yet incomplete, stages of drafting protocols and practices to ensure that clear and measurable goals are established and focused on critical needs regarding improving achievement of individual students.	The school has not attempted to ensure that clear and measurable goals are established and focused on critical needs regarding improving achievement of individual students.

Figure 5.5: Scale for leading indicator 4.1—The school establishes clear and measurable goals focused on critical needs regarding improving achievement of individual students.

Challenges leaders face as they move through the levels of this scale include setting aside time to teach students how to set goals and monitor their progress toward those goals.

Leaders also face a challenge when they encounter the perception that not all students can set goals or that this isn't developmentally appropriate for the youngest learners.

Another common challenge involves managing the *second-order change*, or change that marks a large break from the past (Marzano et al., 2005), associated with this shift. Setting meaningful individual goals for every student is often a very new idea in schools.

Leading Indicator 4.2

The school analyzes, interprets, and uses data to regularly monitor progress toward achievement goals for individual students.

Tracking student progress is part of what school leaders do. Often, they use results from state tests, district benchmark assessments, third-party assessments, and common assessments across grade levels to monitor schoolwide progress. Leading indicator 4.2 requires leaders to take this monitoring a step further to the individual student level. Teachers and building leaders need to monitor individual students' progress to ensure students meet their goals and make an appropriate amount of progress.

Perhaps the most powerful data to regularly monitor, analyze, and interpret come from classroom assessment results. For example, figure 5.6 shows the fourth-grade tracking document from Whiteland Elementary School in Indiana (C. Lewis, personal communication, January 6, 2016). The spreadsheet represents each of the school's students. In addition, each essential standard has a column for the student's baseline (BL) or preassessment score, a column for student achievement after core instruction (Core), and a column for the student's current score (Current). Teachers update the spreadsheet by grade level every couple of weeks. The school's goal is to ensure students reach a proficiency scale score of 3.0 or higher on all the priority standards. This spreadsheet also includes the number of priority standards for which each student has achieved a 3.0 or higher in language arts and mathematics.

# of ELs Mastered	4.RL.2.3 Literature Comprehension	4.RF.5 Oral Fluency	4.RL.2.1 Explicit and Inferred Information	4.RN.2.1 Explicit and Inferred Information	4.RN.2.2 Main Idea and Details	4.RN.3.2 Text Structure	4.RV.2.1 Context Clues	4.RV.2.4 Word Structural Elements	4.W.1 Reading Response and Analysis	4.W.3.2 Informative/ Explanatory Details	4.W.3.2 Introductions	4.W.6.2a Capitalization	EL Average
0	2	2	2.5	2	2	2	2	1.5	2	2	2	2.5	2.04
0	2.5	2	2.5	2	2	2	2	2.5	2	2	2	2	2.13
1	2.5	2	2.5	2.5	2.5	3	2.5	2.5	2	2	2	2	2.33
1	2.5	2.5	2.5	2.5	2.5	3	2.5	2.5	2.5	2.5	2.5	2.5	2.54
2	2	2	2.5	2	2	3	3	2.5	2	2.5	2	2.5	2.33
3	2.5	3	2	3	2	2	3	2	2.5	2	2	2	2.33
3	3	4	3	2	2	2	2	2	2	2.5	2.5	2.5	2.46
3	3	2	2	2	2.5	1.5	2	3	2	2.5	2.5	3	2.33
3	3	3	3	2	2.5	2.5	2	2	2	2	2	2	2.33
4	3	3	3	2	3	2	2	2	2	2	2	2	2.17
4	3	3	1.5	2	3	2	2.5	2	2.5	2	2	3	2.38
4	3	4	2	1.5	2.5	2	2	3	2.5	2.5	2.5	3	2.54
4	3	4	1.5	1.5	2.5	2	2	3	2	2	2	3	2.38
4	3	3	2.5	1.5	2	2	3	2.5	2.5	3	2.5	2.5	2.50
4	3	2.5	2	2.5	3.5	2	2.5	3	2.5	2.5	2.5	3	2.63
4	3	3.5	2	1	2.5	2	1	3	2.5	2	2	3	2.29

Source: Adapted from © 2017 by Whiteland Elementary School.

Figure 5.6: Document for tracking student-level data.

Keeping track of data at this level greatly benefits students. This level of detail makes it easy to see which students need intervention or acceleration by student and by skill, by current level of understanding on each priority standard, and by what they need next. It also makes it easy for staff to monitor knowledge gained, progress in relation to students' individual goals, and triangulation of data with state tests and other third-party assessments. (For additional information regarding the correlation of these types of data with state assessments, see chapter 7, page 176, on leading an HRS at the district level.)

It is important for school staff to monitor individual student progress, but it is equally important for students to track their own progress. Figure 5.7 shows an example of a student progress-tracking sheet used at Break-O-Day Elementary School. The form is quite easy for students to fill out. As they demonstrate that they have achieved a specific competency level on the scale for a specific topic, they simply fill in the bar graph to the appropriate row. (For a detailed description of how students should track their own progress, see Marzano, Norford, et al., 2017.) This sheet becomes part of the data binder described in the previous section on leading indicator 4.1 (page 141).

When a school first begins the process of having students set goals, form plans, monitor progress, and evaluate success, it is normal for the tasks to appear somewhat mechanistic in nature. Monitoring their own progress does not come naturally to all students. Teachers must teach students this process. As students become more comfortable with it and see its value to them personally, they will begin to take more ownership. To fully maximize the possibilities for individual student success in this leading indicator, leaders should look for and cultivate the following student behaviors (adapted from Marzano, 2017).

- Students track their progress and update their status on each of the proficiency scales.
- Students demonstrate pride when they reach their goals.
- Students participate in and enjoy celebrations when they make progress toward or reach their goals.

At some point, leaders must address the issue of report cards, particularly if they want report cards to address both status and growth. The typical report card with a single omnibus grade simply does not suffice. Rather, bar graphs like that depicted in figure 5.7 would always accompany the omnibus grade on a report card. These bar graphs could be an actual part of each report card, or they could be found in supplemental reports. (For detailed examples, see Marzano, 2006, 2010, 2018).

4.C.2a—Mulitplying Multi-Digit by One-Digit Whole Numbers

Level 4	Student can do level 3 and is able to write and solve a real-world situation, creating a one-digit by four-digit problem. Then student must answer the problem and explain how he or she got the answer.
Level 3	Student can multiply a whole number up to four digits by a one-digit whole number and can explain how he or she did it.
Level 2	Student can multiply a one-digit whole number by a two-digit whole number correctly.
Level 1	With help, student can multiply a one-digit whole number by a two-digit whole number correctly.

4	★	★	★	★	★	★
3.5						
3	★	★	★	★	★	★
2.5						
2	★	★	★	★	★	★
1.5						
1	★	★	★	★	★	★
0.5						
	Attempt #1 Date: *8-2-16*	Attempt #2 Date: *9-5-16*	Attempt #3 Date: *9-3-16*	Attempt #4 Date: *11-18-16*	Attempt #5 Date: _____	Attempt #6 Date: _____

Figure 5.7: Student progress tracking sheet.

Lagging Indicators

A school can identify and monitor a lagging indicator for leading indicator 4.2 by establishing that all staff members assist students so 100 percent of the student body monitor progress toward achievement of their goals and evaluate whether they reach their goal in at least one course or subject. Each staff member also shares and discusses examples of three students' progress each semester. They do this so teachers can see how their colleagues track their progress and interact with them about their progress.

Other lagging indicators that address leading indicator 4.2 include:

- Reports, graphs, charts, data walls, or data boards show individual student achievement.

- Teachers regularly report and use results from multiple types of assessments (for example, benchmark and common assessments).
- The school clearly defines protocols or systems for analyzing individual student achievement data.

Quick Data and Continuous Improvement

To collect and analyze quick data for this indicator, a school could, for example, create a data wall that highlights the number of priority standards for which students have reached proficiency. The school can then move students up the wall's learning levels each month as they reach proficiency on additional priority standards.

Other examples of quick data include the following.

- Reports, graphs, charts, data walls, or data boards show individual student achievement.
- Teachers regularly report and use results from multiple types of assessments (for example, benchmark and common assessments).
- Protocols or systems for analyzing individual student achievement data are clearly defined.

Leader Accountability

Leader accountability for this indicator involves monitoring whether programs and practices are in place that lead to data being analyzed and used to regularly monitor progress toward achievement goals for individual students and that these programs and practices are having their desired effects. Leaders can evaluate their effectiveness using the proficiency scale in figure 5.8.

Challenges leaders face as they move through the levels of this scale include creating a system for and gathering individual students' data for each priority standard in each course. This requires establishing an infrastructure that can archive a lot of data at a highly granular level. Also, shifting the data emphasis from external assessments to teacher-created assessments aligned to proficiency scales poses a challenge. Finally, some leaders may lack understanding of why tracking and interpreting individual student progress is so crucial to feedback and learning.

Level 4 Transformations

Level 4 of the HRS model deals with ways of assessing, recordkeeping, and reporting that ensure individual students have readily available information on their current status and level of growth on specific topics. At this level, large changes might occur regarding high-profile topics such as grades, report cards, and transcripts. Although these changes might pose challenges in some situations, they can foster rather dramatically positive results, such as the following.

Sustaining	Applying	Developing	Beginning	Not Attempting
The school continually cultivates information through quick data sources to monitor that data are analyzed and used to regularly monitor progress toward achievement goals for individual students, and it takes proper actions to intervene when quick data indicate a potential problem.	The school has protocols and practices in place to ensure that data are analyzed and used to regularly monitor progress toward achievement goals for individual students, and it can produce lagging indicators to show the desired effects of these actions.	The school has protocols and practices in place to ensure that data are analyzed and used to regularly monitor progress toward achievement goals for individual students.	The school is in the beginning, yet incomplete, stages of drafting protocols and practices to ensure that data are analyzed and used to regularly monitor progress toward achievement goals for individual students.	The school has not attempted to ensure that data are analyzed and used to regularly monitor progress toward achievement goals for individual students.

Figure 5.8: Scale for leading indicator 4.2—The school analyzes, interprets, and uses data to regularly monitor progress toward achievement goals for individual students.

Kelly Faught-McCoy, principal at Grove Valley Elementary, shares the following positive results from Grove Valley Elementary's implementation of level 4 of the HRS model:

After implementing standards-referenced grading and reporting, we have seen steady improvement in the success levels of our students. Our latest state-mandated test scores improved across the board in reading and math 2 to 9 percent, which indicates to us that we are on the right track. (K. Faught-McCoy, personal communication, August 21, 2017)

Grove Valley was also recognized as one of the top public schools in Oklahoma and was identified as a national Blue Ribbon school in the fall of 2017.

At Break-O-Day Elementary School, Trina Lake has seen a shift in student effort as a result of her school utilizing proficiency scales. Regarding the school's work at level 4, Lake says:

> Discussing learning expectations and goal setting has helped our staff and students focus on the next steps to success. It has shifted our focus to a growth mindset versus a fixed mindset. When students know what they need to do, they work harder to reach that next level. Adding in the student goal-setting component has led to greater student pride and success in their learning. Our students track their progress and share what they are learning and how to progress with their parents through student data binders, which are sent home on a regular basis. (T. Lake, personal communication, August 29, 2017)

Principal Jenni Baker at Clark Elementary School in Franklin, Indiana, believes the work her school staff has done at level 4 has increased staff awareness of what students need. Of the HRS model, Baker says:

> Having used a variety of school improvement models over the years, HRS is definitely not one that sits on the shelf. Staff have taken an active role in the process. As a result of the work in level 4, teachers have a better understanding of the learning progression for each concept and skill. This empowers them to create instruction and assessments that enhance learning for all students. Teachers are more involved in collecting data that helps to track student progress on goals, provides direction regarding necessary intervention, and helps to celebrate academic success. As a result of our work on proficiency scales, more students have opportunities to accelerate to above-grade-level skills. (J. Baker, personal communication, September 1, 2017)

Cirsten Lewis at Whiteland Elementary School has seen an increase in teacher collaboration as a result of work at level 4. She states:

> Teachers drove the selection of essential learnings and the creation of proficiency scales. They are the experts in daily execution of the proficiency scales and related assessments. The collaboration of teachers across the district has formerly been nonexistent. Now, teachers are sharing assessments across schools, making adjustments as needed for their own school teams and students. In addition, there exists a new consistency in assessment practices across our schools. The proficiency scales provide clarity as to proficiency and mastery of skills. Conversations during collaborative time within our PLC structure are focused upon quality teaching strategies instead of merely on student data. (C. Lewis, personal communication, September 1, 2017)

Conclusion

Leadership for level 4 of the HRS model focuses on standards-referenced reporting. Such an emphasis directly addresses question 2 of the six critical questions: How will we know if students are learning? It also addresses question 3: How will we respond when students don't learn? This level has two leading indicators. For a school to declare itself highly reliable relative to level 4, leaders must generate lagging indicators for each leading indicator with clear criteria for success. Even after the school has met these success criteria, it must still continue to collect quick data to monitor and react to variations in its performance on the two indicators.

Chapter 6

Competency-Based Education

● ● ●

Level 5 of the HRS model directly addresses question 4 of the six critical questions: How will we extend learning for students who are highly proficient? We think of level 5 of the HRS model as pure standards-based grading. Although this level has similarities to level 4, some distinct differences require specific leadership action for the transition to level 5.

By its very nature, level 5 provides the highest level of reliability for student learning. In level 4, standards-referenced reporting, a student moves to the next grade level or course based on time, usually when a semester or school year ends. In a standards-referenced system, students can move to the next grade level even if they have not demonstrated proficiency in all the priority standards at their current grade level. With level 5, however, that is not the case. In level 5, a competency-based system, students progress to the next grade level only after they have demonstrated proficiency in all the priority standards at their current grade level. In a standards-referenced system, students do not work on content above their grade level. In a competency-based system, students can work on any level of content for which they are ready. This means some students may progress faster than their peers.

Already, many schools incorporate some competency-based practices. For example, a student who surpasses all the mathematics offerings in high school coursework might continue his or her study of mathematics by taking college-level coursework. Numerous schools have implemented this type of opportunity, which represents a competency-based practice. The same can be seen in elementary schools that have advanced reading groups or classes for students who work above grade level. Each of these situations allows students to advance based on their learning and demonstrated level of competence, rather than their seat time.

In addressing the leading indicators for level 5, we will examine strategies a school can use to implement competency-based opportunities systemwide. Although this shift involves a significant change, school leaders can opt to incrementally move to a competency-based approach by designing competency-based pathways for specific content areas, rather than moving to a full competency-based system for all curricular areas right away.

School leaders should also consider that a school could feasibly move directly to a level 5 competency-based system without implementing a level 4 standards-referenced reporting system. However, some of the key components of level 4 are necessary for level 5 to function properly. The most important of these is the development of proficiency scales for priority standards that establish clear and consistent expectations for student competency schoolwide. Also important from level 4 is keeping track of individual students' status and growth and setting goals. Finally, it is important to remember that levels 1, 2, and 3 must provide a solid foundation for levels 4 and 5. A safe, supportive, and collaborative culture (level 1) is bedrock. Effective teaching in every classroom (level 2) provides equity of access to good teaching, and a guaranteed and viable curriculum (level 3) provides equity of access to priority standards.

Proficiency scales are absolutely necessary for this HRS level to function correctly. Scales show students what they must do to demonstrate proficiency, and they allow students to better understand their position in their own development relative to specific standards. Additionally, scales become the guide for developing competency-based assessments that allow students to demonstrate their abilities as they progress through the standards for a specific grade level or course.

In moving to a competency-based system, school leaders must ensure teachers assess competency in a consistent manner and with consistent expectations for students. To this end, school leaders can collect common assessment tasks in an assessment bank, providing teachers and students with multiple consistent opportunities and ideas regarding how to demonstrate competency. Leaders should base these common assessment opportunities on proficiency scales.

For standards that deal with procedural knowledge, such as writing, student portfolios of artifacts can allow students to demonstrate growth and proficiency in these types of skills. Students compile their artifacts that demonstrate progressions of learning to the point where procedural knowledge meets the expectations for proficiency. It would be appropriate for students to present their portfolios for some standards in an oral review format and field questions about their learning from a staff committee. Colleges use this practice to confer master's degrees, and it holds a great deal of potential in a competency-based system, especially at the secondary level. The very nature of teaching in a competency-based format makes oral presentation and review more feasible as an assessment option than in a traditional system.

Level 5 of the HRS model has three leading indicators.

5.1 Students move on to the next level of the curriculum for any subject area only after they have demonstrated competence at the previous level.

5.2 The school schedule accommodates students moving at a pace appropriate to their situation and needs.

5.3 The school affords students who have demonstrated competency levels greater than those articulated in the system immediate opportunities to begin work on advanced content or career paths of interest.

Leading Indicator 5.1

Students move on to the next level of the curriculum for any subject area only after they have demonstrated competence at the previous level.

The language of this leading indicator refers to students not moving to the next curriculum level until they have demonstrated proficiency in all priority standards; it also implies that students can move at a faster pace if they demonstrate competency in all the necessary standards. For that to occur, classroom teaching practices need to look and sound different from traditional classroom teaching practices.

In a traditional classroom, teachers more often engage in information delivery through whole-group lessons and less often provide opportunities for small-group or individualized learning opportunities. In a competency-based classroom, teachers reverse the frequency of those two behaviors. Teachers in a competency-based classroom do less in whole-group instruction and use more facilitated learning approaches. Key competency-based teaching practices include small-group instruction, individualized instruction, and personalized learning. In a competency-based classroom, the teacher does not guard the mountain of knowledge but instead serves as a guide to help students as they climb the mountain. This underscores the need for proficiency scales students can use as a road map for their learning progressions.

In a competency-based system, the scales should reference learning resources students can access to help them engage in a personalized learning approach for specific standards. Figure 6.1 (page 156) shows an example of a proficiency scale that provides a menu of resources students can choose from as they engage in personalized learning opportunities. The standard and the levels of the learning progression appear on the scale's left side, while learning resources related to that specific level of learning appear on the right side.

Measurement Topic: Early Democratic Documents (Grade 10)		
Score 4.0	In addition to score 3.0 content, the student demonstrates in-depth inferences and applications that go beyond what was taught.	**Learning Resources**
		Choice board or menu of student-generated assessments
	Score 3.5 · In addition to score 3.0 content, the student demonstraes in-depth inferences and applications with partial success.	
Score 3.0	The student explains the principles of: • The Magna Carta • The English Bill of Rights • The American Declaration of Independence • The U.S. Bill of Rights The student exhibits no major errors or omissions.	• National Archives website • Library of Congress website • History Channel's *Democracy's Documents*, episodes 1 and 2 • Flipped-classroom video lessons and graphic organizers • Small-group instruction sessions by appointment or request
	Score 2.5 · The student exhibits no major errors or omissions regarding 2.0 content and partial knowledge of 3.0 content.	
Score 2.0	The student exhibits no major errors or omissions regarding the simpler details and processes as he or she: • Recognizes and recalls specific terminology ▪ Constitutional monarchy ▪ Absolute monarchy ▪ Civil rights ▪ Glorious Revolution ▪ John Locke • Performs basic processes ▪ Recall factual statements about the principles of the Magna Carta, the English Bill of Rights, the American Declaration of Independence, and the U.S. Bill of Rights.	• Flipped-classroom vocabulary lesson and vocabulary journal • American history text • *Our Documents: 100 Milestone Documents From the National Archives*

Figure 6.1: Example proficiency scale for personalized learning.

We presented a scale in chapter 5 (see figure 5.1, page 138) that addressed the left-hand side of figure 6.1. The purpose of a proficiency scale is to design and score classroom assessments. That is, teachers use a proficiency scale to create their assessments and score those assessments using the proficiency scale. For details on how to use proficiency scales, see Marzano (2010, 2018). In this figure, we've added a column on the right that lists resources students can use. Most of these resources are online and all can be used by students independently. This is critical to competency-based education—students working on their own without having to wait for the teacher for guidance or permission.

In figure 6.1, we provide resources for score values 2.0, 3.0, and 4.0 only. This is because these are the score values for explicitly stated academic content. The other score values in the scale represent partial knowledge of the content at score values 2.0, 3.0, and 4.0. (For a detailed discussion, see Marzano, 2010, 2018; Marzano, Norford, et al., 2017.) This is also why figure 6.1 does not report score values below 2.0—they have no explicit content associated with them.

Teachers can enhance competency-based instruction by using technology that creates blended-learning opportunities. Students who move at an accelerated pace as well as those who need to revisit content can benefit from blended learning. Although many options for blended learning exist, the flipped-classroom concept suits competency-based instruction well.

School leaders considering a move to a competency-based system may want to have teachers record videos of lessons and archive them for use in the competency-based format. Archiving direct instruction lessons during the early transition to a competency-based system provides teachers with valuable and cost-effective tools for once the transition fully develops. Again, these videos would be part of the content students can access independently. Additionally, if a teacher leaves the school, the school will still have that collection of archived video lessons to use. Ideally, schools should try to accumulate several video lessons dealing with each topic the archive covers so students have the option to choose one or view a few different instructors teach the same topic. In schools where multiple teachers teach the same topic, acquiring a collection of lesson videos for this purpose is simply a matter of planning for the video recording and archiving system.

Lagging Indicators

A school can identify and monitor a lagging indicator for leading indicator 5.1 by having students track their own progress in each standard by using a simple bar-graph sheet. Students can regularly share this sheet with the teacher and their parents.

Other lagging indicators that address leading indicator 5.1 include:

- The school has proficiency scales in place to clearly explain the criteria a student must meet to be considered proficient for each standard at each grade level.
- The school has specific assessments or assessment tasks in place to ensure students have met competency levels for each standard.
- The school has systems in place to report student competency levels.

Quick Data and Continuous Improvement

To collect and analyze quick data for this indicator, a school could, for example, prompt quick checkup conversations in which teachers hold short one-to-one conferences with students, asking them about their current level of progress as they work toward proficiency. Teachers keep a running record of student competency levels that they could periodically review to determine aggregate and individual progress.

Other examples of quick data include the following.

- Students can explain their progress and competency level for specific content areas.
- Teachers can explain how they determine student competency for specific standards in a grade level or content area.
- When asked, parents can explain the system used to report student competency levels.

Leader Accountability

Leader accountability for this indicator involves monitoring whether programs and practices are in place that lead to students moving on to the next curriculum level for any subject area only after they have demonstrated competence at the previous level and that these programs and practices are having their desired effects. Leaders can evaluate their effectiveness using the proficiency scale in figure 6.2.

Challenges leaders face relative to this indicator include not having clear descriptions for student proficiency at each level of the curriculum. In the absence of clear expectations for proficiency, the decision to move students to the next level takes on a great deal of subjectivity.

Sustaining	Applying	Developing	Beginning	Not Attempting
The school continually cultivates information through quick data sources to monitor that systems or protocols are in place to allow students to move on to the next curriculum level for any subject area only after they have demonstrated competence at the previous level, and it takes proper actions to intervene when quick data indicate a potential problem.	The school has protocols and practices in place to ensure that students move on to the next curriculum level for any subject area only after they have demonstrated competence at the previous level, and it can produce lagging indicators to show the desired effects of these actions.	The school has protocols and practices in place to ensure that students move on to the next curriculum level for any subject area only after they have demonstrated competence at the previous level.	The school is in the beginning, yet incomplete, stages of drafting protocols and practices to ensure that students move on to the next curriculum level for any subject area only after they have demonstrated competence at the previous level.	The school has not attempted to ensure that students move on to the next curriculum level for any subject area only after they have demonstrated competence at the previous level.

Figure 6.2: Scale for leading indicator 5.1—Students move on to the next level of the curriculum for any subject area only after they have demonstrated competence at the previous level.

Leading Indicator 5.2

The school schedule accommodates students moving at a pace appropriate to their situation and needs.

This indicator represents one of the most difficult aspects of embracing a competency-based system, because it deals with scheduling, and scheduling practices are deeply ingrained in K–12 education. However, schools have a variety of ways they can accommodate students' moving at their own pace. Blended learning is one of those ways.

Blended learning is the general term for instructional activities that involve both live instruction by a teacher and instruction provided by technology. We addressed aspects of blended learning when we discussed the flipped classroom as well as online resources that should be listed in the right-hand column of a proficiency scale (see figure 6.1, page 156). Blended learning can occur in numerous formats and provides flexibility in many aspects of a school's schedule. It allows students access to the vast majority of technology-based learning tools at any time, and they can progress at a pace that meets both their academic and scheduling needs.

In the transition to a competency-based system, school leaders should provide time and opportunities for teachers to identify blended-learning applications, such as websites, that align with their content standards. As part of this effort, teachers could develop a digital binder of web-based tools and sites from which students can choose. Specific blended-learning tools will also be identified for students on the right side of proficiency scales, as referenced in figure 6.1. For example, LiveBinders (www.live binders.com) is a tool teachers can use to organize Internet resources for specific content topics. This allows students to efficiently view and access these resources for their learning regarding the standard or topic. There are many learning resources available for student or class use online, such as Khan Academy (www.khanacademy .org) or Mr. Math Blog (www.mrmathblog.com).

Using multigrade or multicourse classes also creates opportunities for competency-based learning. In these situations, a teacher has a specific group of students who represent abilities across several grade levels or several different courses within a content area. For example, if a teacher has students from first through third grade and has clear definitions of proficiency in each grade level, then students can openly work on content from the grade level appropriate for their academic needs. Teachers can group and regroup students for small-group instruction based on their current level of proficiency.

In a secondary situation, a teacher might teach a mathematics class that includes algebra and advanced algebra or an English class that includes ninth- and tenth-grade English. A secondary teacher can group and regroup students for different types of small-group instruction or peer learning opportunities.

In multigrade or multicourse classrooms, remember that teachers do not often engage in direct teaching but more often in small-group and facilitated instruction. That is not to say that direct instruction does not occur. At times, a teacher in these classrooms may engage in direct instruction for new content when a large student group is clearly ready for the same topic or standard. However, once students begin to use different learning tools and resources at their disposal, the need for large-group and direct instruction occurs less often and sometimes disappears completely.

Teaming up to work with large groups of students gives teachers another way to create competency-based learning opportunities. As an example, consider an English team that collectively facilitates learning in four different levels of English for multiple learners. The team works with all the students in a variety of time blocks and settings identified in the schedule. These time blocks can include large-group instruction, peer tutoring, small-group instruction, and individual student access to any teacher on the team. Additionally, teacher teams can offer small-group seminars in which each teacher helps students with a predetermined topic or level of learning in a more traditional classroom setting.

Leaders should also empower teams to use blocks of time to create learning opportunities as teachers see needs arise for specific learners. For example, a teacher team might decide to hold a writing lab for students during which the team circulates, answers questions, and provides feedback to individual learners as they write at their appropriate learning level.

Finally, scheduling common content blocks of time can allow students to easily move from one learning level to the next as soon as they are ready. For example, if an elementary school schedules a common reading content block across all grade levels, students can change classrooms to gain a higher level of reading in the curriculum. During this same time, students who need targeted interventions or specific skill development can access teachers who focus specifically on the skills at their level. This type of schedule does not eliminate the use of specific intervention and extension time. In fact, it enhances the school's ability to enact these opportunities with greater flexibility for student needs.

In adapting the school schedule for competency-based learning, school leaders should consider combining several strategies to create a schedule that allows students to move at a flexible pace. Marzano, Norford, Finn, and Finn (2017) provide a variety of options in *A Handbook for Personalized Competency-Based Education*.

Lagging Indicators

A school can identify and monitor a lagging indicator for leading indicator 5.2 by creating a matrix that displays the school schedule's built-in pathways for vertical student movement in different content areas.

Other lagging indicators that address leading indicator 5.2 include:

- Student records or documents indicate individual students work at various learning levels to meet their individual needs in specific content areas.
- The school has individualized learning opportunities in place for students to progress at a pace appropriate to their needs.
- The school has appropriate intervention or remediation opportunities in place for students to access based on their individual learning needs.

Quick Data and Continuous Improvement

To collect and analyze quick data for this indicator, a school could, for example, use student-parent focus groups to gain information about how competency-based schedules and systems work for them. Leaders review and summarize interview information on a systematic basis.

Other examples of quick data include the following.

- Teachers can explain how the school schedule is organized to accommodate individual student needs and progress.
- Teachers can provide specific examples of students moving at a pace appropriate to their individual needs.
- Students can explain their use of individualized learning opportunities that allow them to move at a pace appropriate to their needs.

Leader Accountability

Leader accountability for this indicator involves monitoring whether programs and practices are in place that lead to school schedules being designed to accommodate students moving at a pace appropriate to their situation and needs in all content areas and that these programs and practices are having their desired effects. Leaders can evaluate their effectiveness using the proficiency scale in figure 6.3.

As school leaders move through this scale, they may face the challenge to adjust the daily schedule so instructional time in mathematics occurs at the same time in all grade levels, as does instructional time in reading. This way, they facilitate easy student movement from one learning level to the next in mathematics and in reading. These two content areas are typically considered most critical by educators, parents, and the community because they are the focus of state testing.

Leaders also face a challenge in training teachers to adjust their instruction away from an emphasis on whole-class instruction to an emphasis on small-group and individualized instruction. Finally, the challenge of providing access to quality, blended-learning opportunities for different content areas requires a great deal of slow but methodical development.

Sustaining	Applying	Developing	Beginning	Not Attempting
The school continually cultivates information through quick data sources to monitor that the school schedule is being used to accommodate students moving at a pace appropriate to their situation and needs in all content areas, and it takes proper actions to intervene when quick data indicate a potential problem.	The school has protocols and practices in place to ensure that the school schedule is designed to accommodate students moving at a pace appropriate to their situation and needs in all content areas, and it can produce lagging indicators to show the desired effects of these actions.	The school has protocols and practices in place to ensure that the school schedule is designed to accommodate students moving at a pace appropriate to their situation and needs in all content areas.	The school is in the beginning, yet incomplete, stages of drafting protocols and practices to ensure that the school schedule is designed to accommodate students moving at a pace appropriate to their situation and needs in all content areas.	The school has not attempted to ensure that the school schedule is designed to accommodate students moving at a pace appropriate to their situation and needs in all content areas.

Figure 6.3: Scale for leading indicator 5.2—The school schedule accommodates students moving at a pace appropriate to their situation and needs.

Leading Indicator 5.3

The school affords students who have demonstrated competency levels greater than those articulated in the system immediate opportunities to begin work on advanced content or career paths of interest.

Many secondary schools already have procedures for this leading indicator in place through concurrent enrollment partnerships with postsecondary schools. These options make access to advanced content more prevalent than ever before, and many students take advantage of them. School leaders can and should pursue the same types of opportunities for career-area, internship, and early apprentice training. Multiple reports from the U.S. Bureau of Labor Statistics indicate nationwide labor shortages in skilled trades, such as construction, heating, ventilation, air-conditioning, and refrigeration; information technology; cybersecurity; and health technicians. This information reinforces the need for extended education opportunities in schools, especially secondary schools (Career Education Colleges and Universities, 2016).

The article "Shortage of Skills: Construction and Skilled Trades" (Career Education Colleges and Universities, 2016) states, "This crisis exists because employers demand 'job ready' employees and prospective employees are simply not able to bridge the skills gap without appropriate education and training." School leaders can create an opportunity from this shortage if they develop pathways so students can work on career skills and industry certifications in a competency-based system.

Leaders should also consider creating opportunities for students to move up to secondary-level content even if they are chronologically at lower grade levels. In these types of transitions, proficiency scales become extremely useful and provide the common road map necessary for a seamless transition in learning. For example, a middle school student can begin working on high school–level course content if he or she has access to the proficiency scales for the course and resources to begin learning the content.

Through the use of personalized learning opportunities, a student would not have to change teachers, schools, or classrooms in order to take advantage of this option. With that noted, in some cases, physically moving students is a viable option. For example, if a middle school and a high school share the same campus, students may easily transition between the schools for advanced coursework in specific content areas.

When elementary students move to higher learning levels of content when they are ready, it usually occurs with a single teacher in a single classroom. But schools can take another approach by having grade-level collaborative teams implement strategies for regularly grouping and regrouping learners. *Flexible grouping* is a term to describe these collaborative efforts, and flexible grouping strategies usually occur periodically in a traditional education system. In a competency-based system, flexible grouping is more the norm, as opposed to a periodic intervention approach. In this type of approach, teachers work as grade-level teacher teams, rather than having a class of their own. This allows teachers on a team to focus on a specific group of learners within a content area. Strategies like these lend themselves nicely to competency-based learning, as demonstrated in the following scenario.

A second-grade team of four teachers groups and regroups students for mathematics and reading based on each student's academic progress in the priority standards. The team identifies one member to work with students who progress fast and may, in fact, be ready for work in the third-grade standards before the school year ends. The other three team members work collectively with students needing more time and practice to master the second-grade standards. These three teachers continually group and regroup learners so the teachers can work more efficiently on specific standards with small groups using short, targeted lessons. Students who have success with the content can move to the advanced content group as soon as they demonstrate their readiness to do so. In this system, students move in and between groups at any time based on their academic needs and progress. Because the entire team teaches the content at the same time of day, team members can recognize when a student is ready to move between groups, and they easily facilitate the move.

Lagging Indicators

A school can identify and monitor a lagging indicator for leading indicator 5.3 by keeping a running record of college credits and initial industry certifications earned by students. Each year, leaders set goals for increasing the percentage of students seeking and earning college credits and industry certifications.

Other lagging indicators that address leading indicator 5.3 include:

- The school has documents available to explain different advanced-content options that students can access and work on.
- The school has documents available to explain different options afforded to students for career-path interest studies.
- Individual student records demonstrate which options for advanced content or career interests the students access.

Quick Data and Continuous Improvement

To collect and analyze quick data for this indicator, a school could, for example, meet monthly with community employment partners who offer early apprentice job shadowing and training opportunities for students. The meetings offer the school chances to monitor the success of its students who engage in the program and to gain insight from community partners into how the school can continue to prepare students for these opportunities.

Other examples of quick data include the following.

- Parents can explain different options students can access to work on advanced content.
- Students can describe specific examples of career-path interest studies that the school has available.
- Available data show the percentage of students who are working on advanced content or career-path interest studies.

Leader Accountability

Leader accountability for this indicator involves monitoring whether programs and practices are in place that lead to students who have demonstrated competency levels greater than those articulated in the system being afforded immediate opportunities to begin work on advanced content or career paths of interest and that these programs and practices are having their desired effects. Leaders can evaluate their effectiveness using the proficiency scale in figure 6.4.

Sustaining	Applying	Developing	Beginning	Not Attempting
The school continually cultivates information through quick data sources to monitor that students who have demonstrated competency levels greater than those articulated in the system are afforded immediate opportunities to begin work on advanced content or career paths of interest, and it takes proper actions to intervene when quick data indicate a potential problem.	The school has protocols and practices in place to ensure that students who have demonstrated competency levels greater than those articulated in the system are afforded immediate opportunities to begin work on advanced content or career paths of interest, and it can produce lagging indicators to show the desired effects of these actions.	The school has protocols and practices in place to ensure that students who have demonstrated competency levels greater than those articulated in the system are afforded immediate opportunities to begin work on advanced content or career paths of interest.	The school is in the beginning, yet incomplete, stages of drafting protocols and practices to ensure that students who have demonstrated competency levels greater than those articulated in the system are afforded immediate opportunities to begin work on advanced content or career paths of interest.	The school has not attempted to ensure that students who have demonstrated competency levels greater than those articulated in the system are afforded immediate opportunities to begin work on advanced content or career paths of interest.

Figure 6.4: Scale for leading indicator 5.3—The school affords students who have demonstrated competency levels greater than those articulated in the system immediate opportunities to begin work on advanced content or career paths of interest.

Challenges leaders face as they move through the levels of this scale include finding career-path opportunities for students in specific areas, such as health care. Career-path opportunities are usually limited in number, and access to these can be scarce.

The mechanics of offering dual-credit opportunities on campus can pose a structural challenge if no teachers on staff qualify to teach such courses, because they don't have a content-area master's degree.

Level 5 Transformations

Level 5 of the HRS model deals with a complete paradigm shift in school organization. It completely alters the traditional model of organizing students by grade levels. Students work at their current level of competence in each subject area. Additionally, the HRS model alters the traditional model of every student taking the same amount of time to work through grade-level content. Rather, students take as much or as little time as necessary to move through the content. Following is an example of the results such changes can affect.

> Bill Olsen, principal at Rutland High School in Rutland, Vermont, has seen his school staff embrace the move toward competency-based education, which legislation for their state has set forth:
>
> > As Vermont moves to implement a proficiency-based graduation system by 2020, the systems of Marzano Research provided Rutland High School the tools to build a comprehensive curriculum, instruction, assessment, and reporting infrastructure. Students, parents, and teachers achieve common understanding through clear prioritized standards and proficiency scales. As our high school moves further along this learning continuum, we experience students acquiring a better understanding of what they mastered and what they still need to understand. The Marzano systems facilitate student ownership of the learning, bringing all closer to meeting the goals of our whole-school curriculum. (B. Olsen, personal communication, August 22, 2017)

Level 5 of the HRS model represents uncharted waters for many school and districts. But those who have wholeheartedly ventured into this environment and stayed the course when problems arose have transformed their systems at the very core. Witness the highly successful competency-based systems in Lindsay Unified School in California and Westminster School District in Colorado. Our conversations with Tom Rooney in Lindsay and Superintendent Pam Swanson in Westminster indicate that they believe, as we do, that competency-based education is the rightful future of K–12 schooling.

Conclusion

Leadership for level 5 of the HRS model focuses on competency-based education. Such an emphasis addresses question 4 of the six critical questions: How will we extend learning for students who are highly proficient? The level has three leading indicators. For a school to declare itself highly reliable relative to level 5, leaders must generate lagging indicators for each leading indicator with clear criteria for success. Even after the school has met these success criteria, the school must still continue to collect quick data to monitor and react to variations in the three indicators.

Chapter 7

District Leadership in High Reliability Schools

● ● ●

Although the HRS model is designed as a school-level framework, as shown in chapters 2–6, it can become even more powerful when an entire school district decides to embark on becoming highly reliable. By inference, the same holds true for the PLC process. If district leadership sets its sights on all of its schools operating as high reliability organizations, then it should adhere to the general principles of the PLC process by continually asking the six critical questions, with a few wording changes to reflect the expanded perspective.

As a district:

1. What is it we want students to learn?
2. How will we know if students are learning?
3. How will we respond when students don't learn?
4. How will we extend learning for students who are highly proficient?
5. How will we increase our instructional competence?
6. How will we coordinate our efforts?

We assert that using the five levels of the HRS model is, in fact, the answer to the sixth question. In order to maximize progress in the HRS model, and in turn generate higher levels of student learning, those who work at the district level must make intentional work of balancing districtwide goals and priorities with building-level autonomy. This balance is crucial for a couple of reasons.

First, site-based management approaches of the 1980s and 1990s did not generate higher levels of student performance. At best, school-based management as a strategy for improvement has no discernible effect on student results (Marzano & Waters, 2009). When district leaders leave the school improvement in their purview up to specific schools' individual efforts, they face the harsh reality that some schools increase student achievement year after year, and others do not. Simply, this approach does not lead to high reliability schools across a district.

Second, top-down approaches to school improvement do not typically work very well either. Stakeholders at the school level must actively involve themselves in an improvement effort for it to succeed (Fullan, 2006; Tyack & Cuban, 1997). As Elmore (2006) states, "Internal accountability precedes external accountability and is a precondition for any process of improvement" (p. 114). Forcing schools to progress through external pressures and edicts has not worked and will not work. Furthermore, this approach to school improvement typically leaves schools in worse shape over the long run (Fullan, 2006). If neither site-based management nor top-down change initiatives work well in terms of increasing student achievement, what is the solution?

The most effective school districts have learned valuable lessons from the site-based management wave of education reform and from failed top-down approaches. They have moved to an approach of *defined autonomy* (Marzano & Waters, 2009). In a defined autonomy approach, school districts set district-level goals and non-negotiables, and monitor progress toward those goals. For example, we often see school districts set a goal to improve achievement for all students and close achievement gaps. All schools share the goal but have autonomy in the strategies they choose to reach that goal. When a district engages in the HRS process, schools choose strategies related to the leading indicators for the HRS levels they are working on. (We provide some examples later in this chapter. See "Establish District Roles for Each Level," page 173.) Also, district leaders can take a few general actions to facilitate schools' progress relative to the HRS model. They can set up collaborative teams for building leaders, focus on critical commitments in the HRS model, establish district roles for each level, and celebrate successes.

Set Up Collaborative Teams for Building Leaders

To accelerate progress and ensure long-term commitment to the HRS model, district leadership can set up collaborative teams for building leaders and allocate time for them to meet and interact. This powerful strategy is part of the PLC process. Leaders are part of collaborative teams just like teachers are. When a district seriously commits to becoming highly reliable, it must allow building leaders to come together to discuss the related work. Building administrators shouldn't use this time to simply discuss anything related to the school's operations; they should specifically use this time to focus on the HRS work that occurs in their buildings. Discussions center on new learning in the HRS model as well as on useful products and artifacts of practice for team review. In the appendix (page 185), you will find an example of a principal collaborative team agenda from Clark-Pleasant Community School Corporation in Indiana, where principals have had their own collaborative team meetings focused on HRS work since 2013.

In addition to having discussions about HRS work, a principal collaborative team can help set districtwide goals and priorities for each school year, soliciting valuable feedback from the staff in each school. A key to success with yearly goals and priorities is to limit the number of goals and priorities. The HRS model presents many possible opportunities for priorities. A team must avoid the mistake of biting off too much at once; otherwise, the priorities will not have viability. Including the collaborative team in the process of setting priorities helps balance loose-tight leadership or defined autonomy, as previously described.

Principals who work in districts that provide this collaborative team have indicated their HRS work would be much more difficult, more time-consuming, and slower to accomplish without it. A lot of professional learning occurs with principals and central office staff when everyone talks openly about the challenges each school faces and possible solutions, and then reflects on which strategies worked and which did not in relation to the desired outcomes. Collaboration and sharing of this kind across a district leverage the knowledge and learning from an even larger and potentially more powerful network.

Focus on Critical Commitments in the HRS Model

School districts can offer a variety of supports in the HRS model. But each district has a somewhat different context. As a result, how schools utilize the HRS model and what resonates from district to district will vary. In addition, each leading indicator in each level of the HRS model will be a strength in some schools and districts and a weakness in others. Naturally, the priorities across schools and districts will differ as a result. This makes it clear, however, that schools must adhere to certain critical commitments within each level in order to maximize success because it helps maintain consistent application of the model within schools. Table 7.1 (page 172) lists what we consider the critical commitments leaders must make at each level. We recommend that district-level staff focus on and build support for these critical commitments as each school progresses through the model's levels.

Table 7.1: HRS Model Critical Commitments by Level

Level 1: Safe, Supportive, and Collaborative Culture	• Establish a strong PLC process that involves well-structured collaborative teams and address the six critical questions and three big ideas.

Level 2: Effective Teaching in Every Classroom	• Establish an evaluation system focused on teacher development that:
	  ▪ Is comprehensive and specific
	  ▪ Includes a developmental scale
	  ▪ Acknowledges and supports growth

Level 3: Guaranteed and Viable Curriculum	• Continually monitor the viability of the curriculum. • Create a comprehensive vocabulary program. • Use direct instruction in knowledge application and metacognitive skills.
Level 4: Standards-Referenced Reporting	• Develop proficiency scales for the critical content. • Report status and growth on the report card using proficiency scales.
Level 5: Competency-Based Education	• Get rid of time requirements, and adjust reporting systems accordingly.

Source: Adapted from Marzano et al., 2014.

Districts that have experienced the most success with the model make the critical commitments at each level non-negotiable over time. In other words, these become the *defined* part of the defined autonomy approach. It would typically overwhelm a district to tighten up this much all at once. We recommend that districts accomplish this a level or two at a time over a period of a few years. This type of approach provides the push sometimes needed districtwide without completely overwhelming the system. Figure 7.1 shows the list of non-negotiables for Clark-Pleasant Community Schools.

HRS Level	**Non-Negotiables (Tight)**
Level 1: Safe, Supportive, and Collaborative Culture	• We will have a safe and supportive school environment. • We will have an orderly school environment. • Everyone participates as a member of a collaborative team and embraces the PLC six critical questions, including looking at data in a systematic way and cycling back on all essential learnings.
Level 2: Effective Teaching in Every Classroom	• Each school has a defined language of instruction. • Each staff member self-assesses and sets pedagogical growth goals each year. • Every staff member has the opportunity to see effective instruction, including at minimum participating in at least two instructional rounds per year.

HRS Level	Non-Negotiables (Tight)
Level 3: Guaranteed and Viable Curriculum	• We embrace the notion that all students will learn at high levels. • We provide extra time and support for all students. • We identify essential learnings for each course or grade level. • We align assessments to essential learnings. • Staff ensure they have enough time to teach all essential learnings to mastery. • We created and use a comprehensive vocabulary program. • Direct instruction occurs for knowledge application and metacognitive skills (21st century skills—grades K–5 only for 2015–2016).
Level 4: Standards-Referenced Reporting	• We break down each essential learning into a learning progression (for example, with grades K–7 complete, continue work in grades 8–12). • Progress reporting reflects student growth and essential learning mastery (for example, with grades K–7 complete, continue work in grades 8–12).
Level 5: Competency-Based Education	• Conversations continue regarding what this could look like.

Source: © 2016 by Clark-Pleasant Community Schools.

Figure 7.1: Non-negotiables for Clark-Pleasant Community Schools.

Establish District Roles for Each Level

The five levels of the HRS model imply specific actions from district leaders. Here we consider each of the HRS levels and describe specific items district administrators should be aware of and can do to help schools become highly reliable.

Level 1: Safe, Supportive, and Collaborative Culture

Working to ensure a safe, supportive, and collaborative culture can have strong support at the district level. The most important level 1 non-negotiable from a district perspective is making sure all staff take part on a collaborative team and have time built into the schedule to collaborate on curriculum, instruction, and assessment. A district can achieve this in many ways. One popular approach is a late-start or early-release schedule one day per week. This allows teachers dedicated time for collaboration and collective inquiry. Other common methods to find time to collaborate include common planning or preparation time, before-school time, or after-school time. The way each district addresses this need does not carry as much importance as ensuring it addresses it. Tackling this task individually can challenge schools, so it is an ideal area for district-level staff to step up and provide support to accomplish the task.

In addition to ensuring it has collaborative time in place, the school district can help support school safety by completing campus safety audits. The resources required to accomplish a school safety audit often extend beyond what individual schools have available to them, which can include the time it takes to conduct the audit, the expertise required to do it well, and the knowledge of what should be included. Having somebody who does not work at the building level lead this process also helps ensure bringing another perspective into the process. School staff who work in a building every day can easily overlook things that an outsider might notice.

Level 2: Effective Teaching in Every Classroom

The critical commitment and first area to begin providing district support for level 2 work includes making sure the district puts an evaluation system in place that focuses on growing great teachers. In order to achieve this, the evaluation system must focus on effective pedagogy. The system has to represent what effective teaching looks like. Many districts refer to this as their *language of instruction*. In this way, staff in those districts describe and talk about good teaching.

Typically, districts establish a districtwide common language. If a school district decides to take this path, rather than let each school choose a model of instruction on its own, then it is crucial to have stakeholders from all schools and various teams involved in talking about and deciding on the model's specifics. Otherwise, they will only loosely commit to the model. A common model of instruction will not lead to the desired result of high-quality teaching in every classroom, but stakeholders need to take this first critical step in the process.

Once the district puts a districtwide model of instruction in place, it might provide support in another important area by ensuring all staff have opportunities to see and discuss effective teaching. It can accomplish this in a variety of ways, including through videotaped lessons, instructional rounds, and instructional audits. All of these require resources.

Videotaped Lessons

Districts can help amass videotaped lessons that address the elements included in their instructional model or, at a minimum, set up structures to share videos individual schools collect across a district. It is not as efficient for each school to individually find videotaped lessons or to film them for its staff only. When all schools in a district engage in the sharing process and a district has set up structures for sharing, it requires much less time and effort to see and discuss examples of effective teaching.

Instructional Rounds

We strongly advocate for the use of instructional rounds. Implementing instructional rounds at the school level requires staff to give up valuable time in the school day when they do not have students, or it requires finding coverage for teachers' classrooms while they participate. District-level support can include financial support for substitute teachers so staff can participate in instructional rounds. Schools commonly hire three or four substitute teachers for a day and rotate them through multiple classrooms throughout the day, allowing three to four teachers at a time to participate in instructional rounds. To make this approach work, schools need to allocate fiscal resources for it.

Instructional Audits

A district can also choose to support schools in completing instructional audits. These audits include a triangulation of data from observation scores or videotaped lesson scores, student survey scores, and teacher self-rating scores. Typically, these do not include any evaluation ratings. The main purpose of the audit is not evaluative in nature; rather, it is to give collaborative teams within the building a snapshot of their strengths and their opportunities for growth.

If a district wants to lessen the burden on teachers, it can train a team of observers from across the district on scoring within the districtwide instructional model. We recommend they watch videotaped lessons together, score them, and then have a discussion about the assigned scores to calibrate them as a team of observers. Once the team has completed this and is ready, the school can schedule the observation portion of the instructional audit. This consists of picking a date to do the audit. Often, the building principal will know and coordinate the day, create the schedule of rooms for each observer to go into, and assist district-level staff in organization. The observation team reports to the school on the scheduled day. The team members can simply go into their assigned classrooms and score the lessons they see.

Once they complete scoring, district-level staff can compile the results and generate a report for the school. This would include the strengths and opportunities for growth from the student survey on the instructional model, the staff self-ratings on the instructional model, and the day's observations. This type of approach does not require any additional work from the teaching staff; in fact, in many cases, they do not even know an observer is coming. Instructional audits can create very valuable data for school teams.

Level 3: Guaranteed and Viable Curriculum

District support can greatly enhance success at level 3. The non-negotiables at level 3 from a district perspective include establishing a guaranteed and viable curriculum, establishing a guaranteed vocabulary list and process to teach the terms, setting districtwide goals for student achievement, ensuring all the district's students have access to extra time and support when they need it, and checking that the established guaranteed and viable curriculum correlates with state and national assessments.

The concept of a guaranteed and viable curriculum is pretty straightforward. All students must have the opportunity to learn the critical content, and teachers need the time necessary to effectively teach it. Although it is easy to understand conceptually, creating a guaranteed and viable curriculum can challenge districts for a variety of reasons.

First, historically in many schools and districts, teachers have had complete autonomy to emphasize whatever they want in the content-area standards. Teachers have made that decision one teacher at a time without consistency across classrooms. Tightening this up and asking staff to come to consensus mean giving up some individual autonomy to a broader team of colleagues. Not all teachers find this easy to do.

Second, differing opinions often come up over what teachers should address in the curriculum and to what extent to address it. Conversations about what to teach can surge with passion. If teachers don't use sound criteria to identify the critical concepts in standards documents, the passion-filled debate regarding what to teach and to what degree can turn ugly quickly.

Third, some staff have become accustomed to a coverage mentality. In a coverage mentality, teachers simply race through the curriculum, attempting to cover everything. In our experience, this typically stems from a belief that teachers can address all standards on a standardized test and, therefore, should teach them to an equal degree during instruction. Asking staff members who come from this perspective to prioritize standards as part of developing a guaranteed and viable curriculum leads to fear that students will do poorly on standardized assessments if they consent and move forward.

Schools can overcome these challenges. With support and guidance from district-level leadership, the process becomes much easier. We recommend district leaders organize teacher teams to identify the guaranteed curriculum for each course and grade level. A representative group of teachers from throughout the district should compose these teams. Teams can get input and feedback from their colleagues as the process for identifying essential content begins. They can also take drafts of the guaranteed curriculum back to their colleagues at the school level for additional feedback before making final decisions. Organizing a process like this at the district level allows all stakeholders to provide input. In addition, it ensures the guaranteed curriculum has consistency across a district. Districts can use the same type of process to identify the guaranteed vocabulary for each course and grade level.

Districts should also take the lead on setting districtwide goals for student achievement. Ideally, these would represent both overall performance targets for each content area and specific targets to close any achievement gaps that exist in a district. Once district-level goals are in place, each building can use them as a guide to set its own goals for student achievement. Also, district staff must take responsibility for monitoring progress toward these goals and celebrating success when they achieve them.

Ensuring all students have access to extra time and support when they need it must take place at the building level. When a district is serious about this, it needs to set the expectation at the district level. Schools can find this task challenging. Opportunities for tutoring or extended learning time outside the school day can depend on resources, and not all schools can afford to add those necessary resources.

Some schools and districts must find time in the school day. Many secondary schools establish a zero period in which students can get the help they need. Elementary schools often build specific time into the master schedule for a whole grade level to provide intervention when needed or extensions when students already know the material. District-level staff can provide examples to schools, help find creative ways to restructure time, problem solve, and ensure all schools have the time built in. All these efforts make time more of a variable, which, in turn, shifts the emphasis to student learning.

Finally, district-level leaders need to confirm that the identified and implemented guaranteed and viable curriculum correlates with state and national assessments. They can do this most easily by compiling the number of priority standards with which each student has reached proficiency and running a simple correlation. Building-level leaders don't typically have the knowledge or appropriate statistical software to accomplish this on their own. Even if districts cannot run a correlation, they can see if the data pass the eye test.

For example, table 7.2 (page 178) and table 7.3 (page 179) show the percentage of students who passed the state test in Indiana for Clark-Pleasant Community School Corporation in 2015 and 2016 respectively, based on the number of priority standards with which students had reached proficiency. Without running any statistical tests, looking at the data makes it clear that generally when students reach proficiency on more priority standards, they have a better chance of passing the state assessment. Both tables highlight this. In table 7.2, no students who had proficiency

Table 7.2: Percentage of Students Who Passed the 2015 State Test Who Had Reached Proficiency on Priority Standards

Number of Priority Standards With Which Students Reached Proficiency	Third-Grade Language Arts Pass Percentage	Third-Grade Mathematics Pass Percentage	Fourth-Grade Language Arts Pass Percentage	Fourth-Grade Mathematics Pass Percentage
0	0.0	0.0	0.0	0.0
1	11.1	0.0	12.5	0.0
2	14.3	0.0	25.0	0.0
3	23.1	0.0	57.1	0.0
4	45.0	0.0	20.0	9.1
5	77.8	23.1	40.0	0.0
6	70.6	20.7	52.0	20.0
7	62.2	41.7	65.2	33.3
8	75.0	51.7	73.1	16.7
9	94.4	75.9	66.7	48.3
10	96.8	48.3	88.4	42.9
11	98.3	80.0	81.5	58.3
12	98.3	84.1	94.9	56.0
13		95.6		72.7
14				82.1
15				96.0
16				97.4
Correlation	0.95	0.95	0.94	0.96

Note: All correlations significant at 0.01.

Table 7.3: Percentage of Students Who Passed the 2016 State Test Who Had Reached Proficiency on Priority Standards

Number of Priority Standards With Which Students Reached Proficiency	Third-Grade Language Arts Pass Percentage	Third-Grade Mathematics Pass Percentage	Fourth-Grade Language Arts Pass Percentage	Fourth-Grade Mathematics Pass Percentage	Fifth-Grade Language Arts Pass Percentage	Fifth-Grade Mathematics Pass Percentage
0	24	0	4.4	0	5.9	0
1	25	7.7	12	7.7	13.6	0
2	29.4	0	43.8	0	22.2	13.3
3	60	16.7	56.5	12.5	27	15
4	54.2	18.8	37.5	6.7	35.1	34.8
5	61.9	31.6	64.7	29.2	50	38.1
6	72	17.7	66.7	21.1	74.4	39.1
7	88.9	69	65.6	36	88.9	56.5
8	87.5	54.6	75	40	84.2	68.8
9	82.4	53.3	79.5	56.7	92.7	60
10	95.6	78.4	78	61.8	95.3	70
11	92.9	88.5	97.1	60.6		73.7
12	98.8	97.9		85.3		72.2
13				95.4		87.5
14				100		82.6
15						100
16						100
17						100
18						100
Correlation	0.95	0.95	0.93	0.96	0.98	0.98

Note: All correlations significant at 0.01.

on zero priority standards passed the state exam. Conversely, 94.9 percent of students or more who knew all the priority standards passed the state exam. In addition to the 2015 data, significantly large positive correlations were found in consecutive years (2015 and 2016) between the number of priority standards with which a student was proficient and state test proficiency rates. A 1.0 correlation is a perfect correlation. This would mean that all variance in test scores could be explained by differences in the number of priority standards with which a student had reached proficiency. Correlations greater than 0.9 are very strong. This makes it clear that this district chose the right academic priority standards.

Level 4: Standards-Referenced Reporting

District-level staff can provide valuable support for the work at level 4 that relates to the critical commitments of developing proficiency scales for the essential content and developing a report card that shows status and growth. In addition, district-level staff can help manage the significant second-order change typically associated with level 4 work.

The same teams of teachers described to form a guaranteed and viable curriculum at level 3 can also develop proficiency scales. Districts now have a few options for developing proficiency scales; they can purchase proficiency scales to modify, create proficiency scales from scratch, or implement a hybrid approach.

Purchase Proficiency Scales to Modify

Districts have the option of purchasing existing proficiency scales and then modifying and tweaking them to meet the districts' needs. For example, the state of Maine sells the learning progressions or scales used statewide. In addition, Marzano Research has developed the Critical Concepts proficiency scales that align to the Common Core State Standards and Next Generation Science Standards (see Simms, 2016). Because creating proficiency scales from scratch involves a lot of time, effort, and energy from a team or staff, some districts find this a good option.

Create Proficiency Scales From Scratch

Districts do have the option to create proficiency scales from scratch. Once a district establishes priority standards and a guaranteed and viable curriculum, it is ready for this step. Districts can find resources and books on how to do this readily available online (Marzano, 2010, 2018; Marzano, Norford, et al., 2017).

Implement a Hybrid Approach

A third option for developing proficiency scales is a hybrid approach. With this approach, a district might decide to purchase proficiency scales for some subjects but build its own for other subjects. This is a good option for districts that might struggle with initial attempts to create proficiency scales for a particular subject. It can also work well if districts have tight budgets but desire to see some exemplars as proficiency scale work gets started.

Regardless of which approach a district chooses, the district needs to take the lead in these efforts. A district would find it very difficult to replicate the time, effort, energy, and expertise required to develop quality proficiency scales in every single school. A district-level approach eases the burden.

Staff in the school district must also have the opportunity to make the proficiency scales their own. This carries special importance when staff purchase proficiency scales from another source. They need a keen understanding of what the proficiency scales say, and they need to agree with the learning progression within each. Allowing staff to modify these scales leads to greater commitment to the end product. This commitment to make modifications is crucial regardless of the approach taken when developing proficiency scales.

In addition to developing proficiency scales, district-level leadership also plays a crucial part in developing a report card that illuminates a student's status on priority standards and the growth he or she has made. In chapter 5 (page 146), we discussed report cards that have traditional overall grades but also show students' status and growth via the use of bar graphs. Developing report cards that accomplish this sounds like an easy task; however, in our experience working with schools and districts across the United States, we have found that the student information system companies that provide schools with their report cards can show reluctance to customize such report cards. They typically want schools to use a report card template that they have already set up, and generally, these templates do not show both achievement status and growth. District-level staff are uniquely positioned to push these providers to meet both criteria for a quality report card. For this reason, district-level support is imperative in this area.

In most schools, making changes to reporting structures represents second-order change. We know that changes of this magnitude result in perceptions of a declining school culture, less order, fewer opportunities for input, and decreased communication arising among the school community.

It would be easy to dismiss these perceptions by saying they are just that—perceptions, not the reality. We strongly advise against dismissing them, as in a school community, perceptions serve as some people's reality. Instead, district leaders can constantly remind school staff and leadership that these perceptions normally happen with second-order change. District leaders can mitigate the effects of negative perceptions by focusing constituents' attention on the positive effects produced at levels 1–3 of the HRS model. The same logic applies with level 5.

Level 5: Competency-Based Education

District-level support at level 5 is important for restructuring reporting systems, assisting schools with schedules that allow students to advance when they reach proficiency, getting advanced classes in place, and helping form communication plans with each school community. Reporting systems are never easy to change. Schools need district-level support for these elements for the same reasons they need it with report card changes at level 4. Also, changing school schedules in a competency-based system can pose a challenge. District-level staff can assist schools by gathering and sharing examples from other competency-based schools, helping weigh the pros and cons of different options, and helping decide how to leverage technology to aid in implementation.

The most important level 5 component that district staff can aid in developing is a communication plan. Some communities consider moving to a competency-based system radical. For this reason, a school should inform the entire school community through multiple avenues when it is investigating this shift in school structure. We suggest involving a broad cross section of people in the investigation, including parents, community members, teachers, administrators, support staff, and students when appropriate. When a school makes the decision to move forward with a competency-based system, it helps if this decision comes from a broad-based committee. These individuals can provide valuable perspectives on different people's hopes, fears, concerns, and possibilities.

Celebrate Successes

Working to become high reliability schools and districts involves very difficult and challenging work. Districts cannot forget to celebrate their successes and share them with others. Acknowledging progress toward goals keeps people motivated and moving forward. Obviously, districts should celebrate once they believe they have reached high reliability in each level of the HRS model, but if they celebrate only that, celebrations will occur far too infrequently. Staff members and schools should receive commendation for incremental progress made. When schools find more time for staff to collaborate, they should celebrate. When students receive extra time and extra support for learning, they should celebrate. When staff develop and implement a guaranteed and viable curriculum, they should acknowledge this achievement and celebrate. These are a few examples of the many opportunities for recognition that schools have as they make incremental progress in the HRS model. Although these things alone may not exemplify high levels of student learning, they embody the very work that helps schools and districts achieve more for students.

Conclusion

While the HRS model focuses on the school, districts can use it to stimulate and guide reform throughout the system. If every school in a district is seeking HRS status at some level, district leaders can not only provide support at each level, but also ensure that schools within the system have a certain measure of autonomy in terms of the lagging indicators they create and also a certain level of uniformity simply because they all are following the HRS model.

Closing Thoughts: Rick DuFour's Words

Rick DuFour introduced the discussion of school leadership in his introduction with this question: "Can we be equal and excellent too?" (Gardner, 1961). We, Rick's coauthors, believe as he did that if we put into practice what we know about the PLC process and combine it with what we know about high reliability organizations, we can answer that question with an unqualified *yes*. It is not inconsequential that Rick wrote his introduction at a point in his life when he knew his time was limited. We like to think that Rick saw the merging of his groundbreaking work on the PLC process with the emerging work on high reliability schools as the next significant positive step in K–12 education.

Appendix

Principal Collaborative Team Agenda From Clark-Pleasant Community School Corporation

Priorities for the Year 2016–2017

- Twenty-first century skills
- Student goal setting, planning, and progress tracking
- Proficiency scale development
- Technology use to enhance instruction and electronically deliver parts of lessons to students

Collaborative Team Meeting Norms

- Begin the meeting by adding parking-lot items to discuss after the collaborative meeting ends.
- Begin on time.
- Discuss as a group if extended time is needed.
- Keep conversations confidential unless you seek permission to share.
- Stay fully present.
- Take care of yourself and others.
- Every voice is equal in the conversation, and everyone participates.
- Be nice.
- Hold each other accountable to norms.

8:00–8:05 a.m. Norms Review

8:05–8:45 a.m. Continual Learning

1. Bring information or research on homework, and be prepared to discuss it (for example, see the Harris Cooper, Jorgianne Civey Robinson, and Erika A. Patall [2006] meta-analysis here: http://bit.ly/2my9jHV). Have a discussion about meaningful homework, and cover the following points of discussion.

   - Are we explicitly teaching responsibility and organization?

   - Are there other ways to teach responsibility?

   - Are our expectations realistic for all families?

   - Several of us are interested in checking to see what exactly is being sent home as homework in our buildings.

   - What will our new learning be for the next meeting, and why?

2. Score two videotaped lessons from staff.

   - Have participants watch video of teachers teaching, and score and discuss it.

   - Discuss the possibility of instructional audits. The best instructional audits have three data points.

     a. Teacher self-ratings

     b. Student survey data

     c. Observers' data

   - Watch and score the first video on your own (about forty minutes) before the next PLC meeting and score a second video together at the next meeting.

   - Use an observation form (that the district administration will send to us) while viewing.

   - Ask our instructional coaches about videos they have already used for this purpose.

8:45–10:25 a.m. Sharing

1. Have a product or artifact discussion.

   - Go over the first grading period's essential learning data, by student and skill, and cover the following points of discussion.

     ▪ What are our strengths, and what are our opportunities for growth? Look at these with teams.

     ▪ Look at these for your building as compared to last year's first nine weeks' data.

2. What products or artifacts will we bring to the meeting next month, and why?

   - We won't have time for additional products or artifacts next month.

10:25–10:45 a.m. Implementation Calendar

1. Have we completed the items on our districtwide implementation calendar? How is it going?

2. What is the plan for the next month, the next three months, and the next six months? Expand and make necessary adjustments (see table A.1).

Table A.1: Districtwide Implementation Calendar

Month	Actions	People Responsible
August 2016	• Build specific quick data. • Have all staff do self-ratings on the forty-three elements of the *New Art and Science of Teaching* model.	• Building leaders • All staff
September	• Build specific quick data.	• Building leaders
October	• Build specific quick data. • Gather and compile English Learning (EL) performance for the first quarter.	• Building leaders • Coaches or the building point person
November	• Build specific quick data.	• Building leaders
December	• Build specific quick data. • Have a staff goals update. • Hold elementary scale development committee meetings. • Complete the first round of instructional rounds.	• Building leaders • All staff • Scale development committees
January 2017	• Build specific quick data. • Gather and compile EL performance for the second quarter.	• Building leaders • Coaches or the building point person
February	• Build specific quick data. • Have all staff self-rate on all forty-three elements (professional development day).	• Building leaders • All district staff

continued →

Month	Actions	People Responsible
March	• Build specific quick data. • Gather and compile EL performance for the third quarter. • Have school instructional audit 1.	• Building leaders • Coaches or the building point person • District and building administration
April	• Build specific quick data. • Have school instructional audit 2.	• Building leaders • District and building administration
May	• Build specific quick data. • Compile and share final goal-area self-rating scores. • Gather and compile EL performance for the fourth quarter. • Complete the second round of instructional rounds.	• Building leaders • Coaches or the building point person
June	• Build specific quick data. • Have the Clark-Pleasant Community School Corporation learning summit.	• Building leaders • All staff
July	• Have the HRS summit.	• All staff

10:45–11:00 a.m. Finalization of the Next Collaborative Team Meeting's Agenda

1. Review the "continual learning" and "products and artifacts" for the next meeting.
2. Address any remaining questions.

References and Resources

Ainsworth, L. (2003). *"Unwrapping" the standards: A simple process to make standards manageable.* Englewood, CO: Lead + Learn Press.

Ainsworth, L. (2014). *Common formative assessments 2.0: How teacher teams intentionally align standards, instruction, and assessment* (2nd ed.). Thousand Oaks, CA: Corwin Press.

AllThingsPLC. (n.d.a). *See the evidence.* Accessed at www.allthingsplc.info/evidence on October 10, 2017.

AllThingsPLC. (n.d.b). *Tools and resources.* Accessed at www.allthingsplc.info/tools-resources /search-result/view/id,77 on October 10, 2017.

Amabile, T. M., & Kramer, S. J. (2010). What really motivates workers: Understanding the power of progress. *Harvard Business Review, 88*(1), 44–45.

Autry, J. A. (2004). *The servant leader: How to build a creative team, develop great morale and improve bottom-line performance.* Roseville, CA: Prima.

Battelle for Kids. (2015). *Five strategies for creating a high-growth school.* Accessed at www.battelleforkids.org/docs/default-source/publications/soar_five_strategies_for _creating_a_high-growth_school.pdf?sfvrsn=2 on October 24, 2017.

Bellamy, G. T., Crawford, L., Marshall, L. H., & Coulter, G. A. (2005). The fail-safe schools challenge: Leadership possibilities from high reliability organizations. *Educational Administration Quarterly, 41*(3), 383–412.

Boston Consulting Group. (2014, December). *Teachers know best: Teachers' views on professional development.* Seattle, WA: Bill and Melinda Gates Foundation. Accessed at http://k12education. gatesfoundation.org/wp-content/uploads/2015/04/Gates -PDMarketResearch-Dec5.pdf on October 24, 2017.

Bourrier, M. (2011). *The legacy of the theory of high reliability organizations: An ethnographic endeavor* (Working Paper No. 6). Geneva, Switzerland: Université de Genève.

Brookover, W. B. (1979). *School social systems and student achievement: Schools can make a difference.* New York: Praeger.

Brookover, W. B., & Lezotte, L. W. (1979). *Changes in school characteristics coincident with changes in student achievement.* East Lansing: Institute for Research on Teaching, Michigan State University. (ERIC Document Reproduction Service No. ED181005)

Buckingham, M. (2005). *The one thing you need to know: . . . About great managing, great leading, and sustained individual success.* New York: Free Press.

Carbaugh, B. G., Marzano, R. J., & Toth, M. D. (2015). *School leadership for results: Shifting the focus of leader evaluation.* West Palm Beach, FL: Learning Sciences International.

Career Education Colleges and Universities. (2016, July 8). *Shortage of skills: Construction and skilled trades*. Accessed at www.career.org/news/shortage-of-skills-construction-skilled-trades on October 10, 2017.

Chenoweth, K. (2009). It can be done, it's being done, and here's how. *Phi Delta Kappan, 91*(1), 38–43.

Christman, J. B., Neild, R. C., Bulkley, K. E., Blanc, S., Liu, R., Mitchell, C. A., & Travers, E. (2009, June). *Making the most of interim assessment data: Lessons from Philadelphia*. Philadelphia: Research for Action. Accessed at www.researchforaction.org/making-the-most-of-interim-assessment-data -lessons-from-philadelphia on October 24, 2017.

Collins, J. (2001). *Good to great: Why some companies make the leap . . . and others don't*. New York: HarperBusiness.

Conzemius, A. E., & O'Neill, J. (2014). *The handbook for SMART school teams: Revitalizing best practices for collaboration* (2nd ed.). Bloomington, IN: Solution Tree Press.

Cooper, H., Robinson, J. C., & Patall, E. A. (2006). Does homework improve academic achievement? A synthesis of research, 1987–2003. *Review of Educational Research, 76*(1), 1–62.

Cotton, K. (2003). *Principals and student achievement: What the research says*. Alexandria, VA: Association for Supervision and Curriculum Development.

Cuban, L. (1992). Managing dilemmas while building professional communities. *Educational Researcher, 21*(1), 4–11.

Deal, T. E., & Kennedy, A. A. (1983). Culture and school performance. *Educational Leadership, 40*(5), 14–15.

Donmoyer, R. (1985). Cognitive anthropology and research on effective principals. *Educational Administration Quarterly, 22*, 31–57.

DuFour, R., DuFour, R., & Eaker, R. (2008). *Revisiting Professional Learning Communities at Work: New insights for improving schools*. Bloomington, IN: Solution Tree Press.

DuFour, R., DuFour, R., Eaker, R., & Karhanek, G. (2004). *Whatever it takes: How professional learning communities respond when kids don't learn*. Bloomington, IN: Solution Tree Press.

DuFour, R., DuFour, R., Eaker, R., & Many, T. (2010). *Learning by doing: A handbook for Professional Learning Communities at Work* (2nd ed.). Bloomington, IN: Solution Tree Press.

DuFour, R., DuFour, R., Eaker, R., Many, T. W., & Mattos, M. (2016). *Learning by doing: A handbook for Professional Learning Communities at Work* (3rd ed.). Bloomington, IN: Solution Tree Press.

DuFour, R., & Eaker, R. (1998). *Professional Learning Communities at Work: Best practices for enhancing student achievement*. Bloomington, IN: Solution Tree Press.

DuFour, R., & Fullan, M. (2013). *Cultures built to last: Systemic PLCs at Work*. Bloomington, IN: Solution Tree Press.

DuFour, R., & Marzano, R. J. (2011). *Leaders of learning: How district, school, and classroom leaders improve student achievement*. Bloomington, IN: Solution Tree Press.

Duke, D. (1982). Leadership functions and instructional effectiveness. *NASSP Bulletin, 66*, 5–9.

Eaker, R., & Sells, D. (2016). *A new way: Introducing higher education to Professional Learning Communities at Work*. Bloomington, IN: Solution Tree Press.

Edmonds, R. R. (1979). Effective schools for the urban poor. *Educational Leadership, 37*(1), 15–18, 20–24.

Edmonds, R. R. (1982). *Programs of school improvement: An overview*. Washington, DC: National Institute of Education.

Elmore, R. F. (2003). *Knowing the right thing to do: School improvement and performance-based accountability*. Washington, DC: National Governors Association Center for Best Practices. Accessed at www.nga.org/files/live/sites/NGA/files/pdf/0803KNOWING.pdf on October 10, 2017.

Elmore, R. F. (2006). *School reform from the inside out: Policy, practice, and performance*. Cambridge, MA: Harvard Education Press.

Elmore, R. F. (2010). "I used to think . . . and now I think . . ." *Harvard Education Letter, 26*(1), 7–8.

Elmore, R. F., & City, E. (2007). The road to school improvement. *Harvard Education Letter, 23*(3). Accessed at www.hepg.org/hel/article/229#home on October 24, 2017.

Ericsson, K. A., & Charness, N. (1994). Expert performance: Its structure and acquisition. *American Psychologist, 49*(8), 725–747.

Ericsson, K. A., Krampe, R. T., & Tesch-Romer, C. (1993). The role of deliberate practice in the acquisition of expert performance. *Psychological Review, 100*(3), 363–406.

Every Student Succeeds Act of 2015, Pub. L. No. 114–95 § 114 Stat. 1177 (2015–2016).

Fairman, M. F., & McLean, L. (2003). *Enhancing leadership effectiveness: Strategies for establishing and maintaining effective schools.* Lenexa, KS: Joshua.

Flanagan, T., Grift, G., Lipscombe, K., Sloper, C., & Wills, J. (2016). *Transformative collaboration: Five commitments for leading a professional learning community.* Cheltenham, Victoria, Australia: Hawker Brownlow Education.

Fullan, M. (2001). *Leading in a culture of change.* San Francisco: Jossey-Bass.

Fullan, M. (2006, November). *Change theory: A force for school improvement* (Seminar Series Paper No. 157). East Melbourne, Victoria, Australia: Centre for Strategic Education.

Gallimore, R., Ermeling, B. A., Saunders, W. M., & Goldenberg, C. (2009). Moving the learning of teaching closer to practice: Teacher education implications of school-based inquiry teams. *Elementary School Journal, 109*(5), 537–553.

Gallup. (2014). *The state of America's schools: The path to winning again in education.* Washington, DC: Author.

Gardner, J. W. (1961). *Excellence: Can we be equal and excellent too?* New York: Harper.

Gladwell, M. (2002). *The tipping point: How little things can make a big difference.* Boston: Back Bay Books.

Glenn, B. C., & McLean, T. (1981). *What works? An examination of effective schools for poor black children.* Boston: Center for Law and Education.

Goddard, R. D., Hoy, W. K., & Hoy, A. W. (2004). Collective efficacy beliefs: Theoretical developments, empirical evidence, and future directions. *Educational Researcher, 33*(3), 3–13.

Hattie, J. (2009). *Visible learning: A synthesis of over 800 meta-analyses relating to achievement.* New York: Routledge.

Hattie, J. (2012). *Visible learning for teachers: Maximizing impact on learning.* New York: Routledge.

Hattie, J. (2015). The applicability of visible learning to higher education. *Scholarship of Teaching and Learning in Psychology, 1*(1), 79–91.

Haycock, K. (1998). Good teaching matters: How well-qualified teachers can close the gap. *Thinking K–16, 3*(2), 1–14.

Heath, C., & Heath, D. (2010). *Switch: How to change things when change is hard.* New York: Broadway Books.

Heflebower, T., Hoegh, J. K., & Warrick, P. (2014). *A school leader's guide to standards-based grading.* Bloomington, IN: Marzano Research.

Heifetz, R. A. (1994). *Leadership without easy answers.* Cambridge, MA: Belknap Press of Harvard University Press.

Heifetz, R. A., & Laurie, D. L. (2001). The work of leadership. *Harvard Business Review, 79*(11), 131–140.

Herman, R., Gates, S. M., Arifkhanova, A. Barrett, M., Bega, A. Chavez-Herrerias, E. R., et al. (2016). *School leadership interventions under the Every Student Succeeds Act: Evidence review: Updated and expanded.* Santa Monica, CA: The RAND Corporation.

Hitt, D. H., & Tucker, P. D. (2016). Systematic review of key leader practices found to influence student achievement: A unified framework. *Review of Educational Research, 86*(2), 531–569.

Hord, S. M. (1997). *Professional learning communities: Communities of continuous inquiry and improvement.* Austin, TX: Southwest Educational Development Laboratory.

Katzenbach, J. R., & Smith, D. K. (1993). *The wisdom of teams: Creating the high-performance organization*. Boston: Harvard Business School Press.

Kotter, J. P., & Cohen, D. S. (2002). *The heart of change: Real-life stories of how people change their organizations*. Boston: Harvard Business School Press.

Kraft, M. A., & Gilmour, A. F. (2017). Revisiting the widget effect: Teacher evaluation reforms and the distribution of teacher effectiveness. *Educational Researcher, 46*(5), 234–249.

Leithwood, K. (1994). Leadership for school restructuring. *Educational Administration Quarterly, 30*(4), 498–518.

Little, J. W. (2006, December). *Professional community and professional development in the learning-centered school*. Washington, DC: National Education Association. Accessed at www.nea.org/assets/docs/HE/mf_pdreport.pdf on October 24, 2017.

Louis, K. S., Leithwood, K., Wahlstrom, K. L., & Anderson, S. E. (2010, July). *Investigating the links to improved student learning: Final report of research findings*. Minneapolis: University of Minnesota, Center for Applied Research and Educational Improvement. Accessed at www.wallacefoundation.org/knowledge-center/Documents/Investigating-the-Links-to-Improved-Student-Learning.pdf on October 11, 2017.

Louis, K. S., Marks, H. M., & Kruse, S. D. (1996). Teachers' professional community in restructuring schools. *American Educational Research Journal, 33*(4), 757–798.

Marzano, R. J. (2001). *A new era of school reform: Going where the research takes us*. Aurora, CO: Mid-Continent Research for Education and Learning.

Marzano, R. J. (2003). *What works in schools: Translating research into action*. Alexandria, VA: Association for Supervision and Curriculum Development.

Marzano, R. J. (2006). *Classroom assessment and grading that work*. Alexandria, VA: Association for Supervision and Curriculum Development.

Marzano, R. J. (2009). Setting the record straight on "high-yield" strategies. *Phi Delta Kappan, 91*(1), 30–37.

Marzano, R. J. (2010). *Formative assessment and standards-based grading*. Bloomington, IN: Marzano Research.

Marzano, R. J. (2011). The art and science of teaching / making the most of instructional rounds. *Educational Leadership, 68*(5), 80–81.

Marzano, R. J. (2012). *Becoming a reflective teacher*. Bloomington, IN: Marzano Research.

Marzano, R. J. (2017). *The new art and science of teaching*. Bloomington, IN: Solution Tree Press.

Marzano, R. J. (2018). *Making classroom assessments reliable and valid*. Bloomington, IN: Solution Tree Press.

Marzano, R. J. (in press). *The research base for the High Reliability Schools model*. Centennial, CO: Marzano Research.

Marzano, R. J., Brandt, R. S., Hughes, C. S., Jones, B. F., Presseisen, B. Z., Rankin, S. C., & Suhor, C. (1988). *Dimensions of thinking: A framework for curriculum and instruction*. Alexandria, VA: Association for Supervision and Curriculum Development.

Marzano, R. J., Frontier, T., & Livingston, D. (2011). *Effective supervision: Supporting the art and science of teaching*. Alexandria, VA: Association for Supervision and Curriculum Development.

Marzano, R. J., & Heflebower, T. (2012). *Teaching and assessing 21st century skills*. Bloomington, IN: Marzano Research.

Marzano, R. J., Heflebower, T., Hoegh, J. K., Warrick, P., & Grift, G. (2016). *Collaborative teams that transform schools: The next step in PLCs*. Bloomington, IN: Marzano Research.

Marzano, R. J., Norford, J. S., Finn, M., & Finn, D., III. (2017). *A handbook for personalized competency-based education*. Bloomington, IN: Marzano Research.

Marzano, R. J., Scott, D., Boogren, T. H., & Newcomb, M. L. (2017). *Motivating and inspiring students: Strategies to awaken the learner*. Bloomington, IN: Marzano Research.

Marzano, R. J., & Simms, J. A. (2013). *Coaching classroom instruction*. Bloomington, IN: Marzano Research.

Marzano, R. J., & Toth, M. D. (2013). *Teacher evaluation that makes a difference: A new model for teacher growth and student achievement.* Alexandria, VA: Association for Supervision and Curriculum Development.

Marzano, R. J., Warrick, P., & Simms, J. A. (2014). *A handbook for high reliability schools: The next step in school reform.* Bloomington, IN: Marzano Research.

Marzano, R. J., & Waters, T. (2009). *District leadership that works: Striking the right balance.* Bloomington, IN: Solution Tree Press.

Marzano, R. J., Waters, T., & McNulty, B. A. (2005). *School leadership that works: From research to results.* Alexandria, VA: Association for Supervision and Curriculum Development.

Maslow, A. H. (1943). A theory of human motivation. *Psychological Review, 50*(4), 370–396.

Maslow, A. H. (1954). *Motivation and personality.* New York: Harper & Row.

McLaughlin, M. W. (1993). What matters most in teachers' workplace context? In J. W. Little & M. W. McLaughlin (Eds.), *Teachers' work: Individuals, colleagues, and contexts* (pp. 79–103). New York: Teachers College Press.

National Governors Association Center for Best Practices & Council of Chief State School Officers. (2010). *Common Core State Standards for English language arts and literacy in history/social studies, science, and technical subjects.* Washington, DC: Authors. Accessed at www.corestandards.org /assets/CCSSI_ELA%20Standards.pdf on December 12, 2017.

North Highland. (2014). *Principles of high reliability organizations.* Atlanta: Author.

Nye, B., Konstantopoulos, S., & Hedges, L. V. (2004). How large are teacher effects? *Educational Evaluation and Policy Analysis, 26*(3), 237–257.

Odden, A. R., & Archibald, S. J. (2009). *Doubling student performance . . . and finding the resources to do it.* Thousand Oaks, CA: Corwin Press.

Patterson, K., Grenny, J., Maxfield, D., McMillan, R., & Switzler, A. (2008). *Influencer: The power to change anything.* New York: McGraw-Hill.

Popham, W. J. (2013). Formative assessment's "advocatable moment." *Education Week, 32*(15), 29.

Purkey, W. W. (1991). *What is invitational education and how does it work?* Paper presented at the annual California State Conference on Self-Esteem, Santa Clara, CA.

Purkey, W. W., & Novak, J. M. (1988). *Education: By invitation only.* Bloomington, IN: Phi Delta Kappa.

Purkey, W. W., & Novak, J. M. (1996). *Inviting school success: A self-concept approach to teaching, learning, and democratic process* (3rd ed.). Belmont, CA: Wadsworth.

Rath, T., & Clifton, D. O. (2005). *How full is your bucket?: Positive strategies for work and life.* New York: Gallup Press.

Recognize. (n.d.). In *Thesaurus.com.* Accessed at www.thesaurus.com/browse/recognize on October 24, 2017.

Reeves, D. B. (2004). *Accountability for learning: How teachers and school leaders can take charge.* Alexandria, VA: Association for Supervision and Curriculum Development.

Robinson, M. A., Passantino, C., Acerra, M., Bae, L., Tiehen, K., Pido, E., et al. (2010, November). *School perspectives on collaborative inquiry: Lessons learned from New York City, 2009–2010.* Philadelphia: Consortium for Policy Research in Education.

Rosenholtz, S. J. (1991). *Teachers' workplace: The social organization of schools.* New York: Teachers College Press.

Saphier, J., King, M., & D'Auria, J. (2006). Three strands form strong school leadership. *Journal of Staff Development, 27*(2), 51–57.

Schneider, M. C., Egan, K. L., & Julian, M. W. (2013). Classroom assessment in the context of high-stakes testing. In J. H. McMillan (Ed.), *SAGE handbook of research on classroom assessment* (pp. 55–70). Thousand Oaks, CA: SAGE.

Schön, D. A. (1983). *The reflective practitioner: How professionals think in action.* New York: Basic Books.

Senninger, T. (2000). *Abenteuer leiten—in Abenteuern lernen.* Münster, Germany: Ökotopia.

Sergiovanni, T. J. (2004). Building a community of hope. *Educational Leadership, 61*(8), 33–38.

Simms, J. A. (2016, August 8). *The critical concepts.* Centennial, CO: Marzano Research. Accessed at www.marzanoresearch.com/research/reports/the-critical-concepts on October 5, 2017.

Stenhouse, L. (1975). *Introduction to curriculum research and development.* London: Heinemann Educational.

Stigler, J. W., & Hiebert, J. (2009). Closing the teaching gap. *Phi Delta Kappan, 91*(3), 32–37.

Strauss, V. (2013, July 25). Answer sheet: How much time do school districts spend on standardized testing? This much. *The Washington Post.* Accessed at www.washingtonpost.com/news/answer -sheet/wp/2013/07/25/how-much-time-do-school-districts-spend-on-standardized-testing-this -much/?utm_term=.fe22ad1e1b98 on October 10, 2017.

Stringfield, S. (1995). Attempting to enhance students' learning through innovative programs: The case for schools evolving into high reliability organizations. *School Effectiveness and School Improvement, 6*(1), 67–96.

Stringfield, S., & Datnow, A. (2002). Systemic supports for schools serving students placed at risk. *Yearbook of the National Society for the Study of Education, 101*(2), 269–288.

ThemPra Social Pedagogy. (n.d.). *The learning zone model.* Accessed at www.thempra.org.uk/social -pedagogy/key-concepts-in-social-pedagogy/the-learning-zone-model on October 10, 2017.

Toch, T., & Rothman, R. (2008). *Rush to judgment: Teacher evaluation in public education.* Washington, DC: Education Sector.

Tyack, D., & Cuban, L. (1997). *Tinkering toward utopia: A century of public school reform.* Cambridge, MA: Harvard University Press.

U.S. Department of Education. (2010, March). *A blueprint for reform: The reauthorization of the Elementary and Secondary Education Act.* Washington, DC: U.S. Department of Education, Office of Planning, Evaluation and Policy Development.

U.S. Department of Education. (2017). *Every Student Succeeds Act (ESSA).* Accessed at www.ed.gov/essa ?src=rn%20Retrieved%20August%203,%202017 on October 11, 2017.

Weber, G. (1971). *Inner-city children can be taught to read: Four successful schools* (CBE Occasional Papers No. 18). Washington, DC: Council for Basic Education.

Wei, R. C., Darling-Hammond, L., Andree, A., Richardson, N., & Orphanos, S. (2009, February). *Professional learning in the learning profession: A status report on teacher development in the U.S. and abroad.* Dallas, TX: National Staff Development Council.

Weick, K. E., & Sutcliffe, K. M. (2007). *Managing the unexpected: Resilient performance in an age of uncertainty* (2nd ed.). San Francisco: Jossey-Bass.

Weick, K. E., Sutcliffe, K. M., & Obstfeld, D. (1999). Organizing for high reliability: Processes of collective mindfulness. *Research in Organizational Behavior, 1*, 81–123.

Weisberg, D., Sexton, S., Mulhern, J., & Keeling, D. (2009). *The widget effect: Our national failure to acknowledge and act on differences in teacher effectiveness* (2nd ed.). Brooklyn, NY: The New Teacher Project.

Wiggins, G., & McTighe, J. (2007). *Schooling by design: Mission, action, and achievement.* Alexandria, VA: Association for Supervision and Curriculum Development.

Wiliam, D., & Thompson, M. (2007). Integrating assessment with learning: What will it take to make it work? In C. A. Dwyer (Ed.), *The future of assessment: Shaping teaching and learning* (pp. 53–82). Mahwah, NJ: Erlbaum.

Wright, S. P., Horn, S. P., & Sanders, W. L. (1997). Teacher and classroom context effects on student achievement: Implications for teacher evaluation. *Journal of Personnel Evaluation in Education, 11*(1), 57–67.

Youngs, P., & King, M. B. (2002). Principal leadership for professional development to build school capacity. *Educational Administration Quarterly, 38*(5), 643–670.

Index

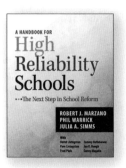

A Handbook for High Reliability Schools
Robert J. Marzano, Phil Warrick, and Julia A. Simms

Transform your schools into organizations that take proactive steps to ensure student success. Using a research-based, five-level hierarchy along with leading and lagging indicators, you'll learn to assess, monitor, and confirm the effectiveness of your schools.

BKL020

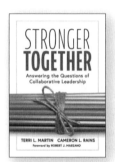

Stronger Together
Terri L. Martin and Cameron L. Rains

How do I build collaborative teams that support a common vision? How do I tap into others' skills? New and veteran leaders ask themselves these questions. *Stronger Together* will help you face your current reality and determine steps for improvement.

BKF792

Every School, Every Team, Every Classroom
Robert Eaker and Janel Keating

The PLC journey begins with a dedication to ensuring the learning of every student. Using many examples and reproducible tools, the authors explain the need to focus on creating simultaneous top-down and bottom-up leadership. Learn how to grow PLCs by encouraging innovation at every level.

BKF534

Learning by Doing, 3rd Edition
Richard DuFour, Rebecca DuFour, Robert Eaker, Thomas W. Many, and Mike Mattos

Discover how to transform your school or district into a high-performing PLC. The third edition of this comprehensive action guide offers new strategies for addressing critical PLC topics, including hiring and retaining new staff, creating team-developed common formative assessments, and more.

BKF746

Solution Tree | Press

a division of

Solution Tree

Visit SolutionTree.com or call 800.733.6786 to order.

GL⬤BAL PD

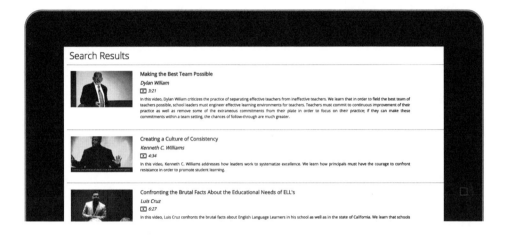

Access **Hundreds of Videos & Books** from Top Experts

Global PD gives educators focused and goals-oriented training from top experts. You can rely on this innovative online tool to improve instruction in every classroom.

- Gain job-embedded PD from the largest library of PLC videos and books in the world.

- Customize learning based on skill level and time commitments; videos are less than 20 minutes, and books can be browsed by chapter to accommodate busy schedules.

- Get unlimited, on-demand access—24 hours a day.

 Solution Tree